WHITAKER'S ALMANACK SPORT QUIZ BOOK

D1140301

A&C BLACK PUBLISHERS
LONDON

A & C Black Publishers Ltd
36 Soho Square, London W1D 3QY

Whitaker's Almanack published annually since 1868

© 2010 A & C Black Publishers Ltd

ISBN 978-1-4081-2246-4

Cover image © Shutterstock

Typeset in the UK by RefineCatch Ltd, Bungay, Suffolk NR35 1EF
Printed in the UK by Cox & Wyman, Cardiff Road, Reading, Berkshire RG1 8EX

Whitaker's is a Registered trade mark of J. Whitaker and Sons Ltd, Registered Trade Mark Nos. (UK) 1322125/09; 13422126/16 and 1322127/41; (EU) 19960401/09, 16, 41, licensed for use by A & C Black Publishers Ltd.

The publishers make no representation, express or implied, with regard to the accuracy of the information contained in this book and cannot accept legal responsibility for any errors or omissions that take place.

This book is produced using paper that is made from wood grown in managed, sustainable forests. It is natural, renewable and recyclable. The logging and manufacturing processes conform to the environmental regulations of the country of origin.

A CIP catalogue record for this book is available from the British Library.

Editorial Staff
Questions by: Phil Ascough, Trevor Bugg
Project Editor: Ruth Craven
Editors: Ross Fulton, Matt Munday, Ruth Northey, Clare Slaven
Publisher (Yearbooks): Claire Fogg

CONTENTS

FOOTBALL

PREMIER LEAGUE

---

1 Who scored the first-ever goal in the Premier League?

a) Teddy Sheringham

b) Andy Cole

c) Brian Deane

---

2 As well as Crystal Palace, which club played Premier League 'home' games at Selhurst Park during the 1993–4 season?

a) Wimbledon

b) Fulham

c) Charlton Athletic

---

3 Which goalkeeper has made the most appearances in the history of the Premier League?

a) Mark Schwarzer

b) David James

c) Brad Friedel

---

4 Which Premier League club's official crest includes a Latin motto which translates as 'Pride In Battle'?

a) Aston Villa

b) Manchester City

c) Tottenham Hotspur

---

5 For the first time, all three promoted clubs avoided relegation in 2001–2. The clubs were Bolton Wanderers, Blackburn Rovers and which other side?

a) Fulham

b) Queens Park Rangers

c) Ipswich Town

6 In 2008, which team were promoted to the Premier League, reaching the top division for the first time in their history?

a) Watford

b) Burnley

c) Hull City

7 In a 2007 Premier League game between Portsmouth and Reading, 11 goals were scored. What was the final score?

a) Portsmouth 9, Reading 2

b) Portsmouth 7, Reading 4

c) Portsmouth 5, Reading 6

8 Alan Shearer is the Premier League's all-time leading scorer with how many goals?

a) 173

b) 207

c) 260

9 Who was the manager of Manchester City when they returned to the Premier League in 2002?

a) Joe Royle

b) Kevin Keegan

c) Stuart Pearce

10 In 1992 there were 22 Premier League clubs. How many of these remained members up to and including the 2009–10 season?

a) Three

b) Five

c) Seven

A

1	c
2	a
3	b
4	b
5	a
6	c
7	b
8	c
9	b
10	c

BRITS ABROAD

1 Former England manager Glenn Hoddle played for which club in France's Ligue 1?

a) Paris Saint-Germain

b) AS Monaco

c) RC Lens

2 Wales legend John Charles joined which Italian club in 1957?

a) AC Milan

b) Torino

c) Juventus

3 Ron Atkinson became manager of which Spanish club in 1988?

a) Atlético Madrid

b) Sevilla

c) Málaga

4 After stepping down as England manager in 1990, Sir Bobby Robson took over at which Dutch club?

a) Ajax

b) PSV Eindhoven

c) Feyenoord

5 Which Australian A-League club did Robbie Fowler join in 2009?

a) North Queensland Fury

b) Melbourne Victory

c) Central Coast Mariners

6 While with Real Madrid, in which year did Steve McManaman win a Champions League winners' medal?

a) 1998

b) 2000

c) 2003

7 Which England international joined AC Milan in June 1961?

a) Gerry Hitchens

b) Peter Swan

c) Jimmy Greaves

8 Dean Saunders scored the winning goal in the 1996 Turkish Cup final for which club?

a) Fenerbahce

b) Besiktas

c) Galatasaray

9 Apart from Switzerland and Finland, Roy Hodgson has been the head coach of which national team?

a) United Arab Emirates

b) Japan

c) Australia

10 Leyton-born Colin Kazim-Richards played for which country at the 2008 European Championships?

a) Belgium

b) Germany

c) Turkey

A

1 b

2 c

3 a

4 b

5 a

6 b

7 c

8 c

9 a

10 c

WORLD CUP – PART 1

1 Which country co-hosted the finals with South Korea in 2002?

a) North Korea

b) Japan

c) China

2 Which team won the first World Cup in 1930?

a) Argentina

b) Uruguay

c) Italy

3 Brazil player Jairzinho established which World Cup finals record in 1970?

a) Scored most goals in a tournament

b) Scored in every game of every round

c) First player to be sent off

4 Which player replaced Gordon Banks, who was ill, in the England goal for their quarter-final against West Germany in Mexico in 1970?

a) Peter Bonetti

b) Gordon West

c) Peter Shilton

5 During the 1994 final in Los Angeles, which Italian player took – and missed – the final penalty in the shoot-out against Brazil?

a) Franco Baresi

b) Nicola Berti

c) Roberto Baggio

6 Which English referee was in charge of the infamous Battle of Santiago between Chile and Italy in 1962?

a) Ken Aston

b) Arthur Ellis

c) Stanley Rous

7 What was the nickname of Germany's World Cup-winning captain and manager Franz Beckenbauer?

a) The General

b) The Prince

c) The Kaiser

8 In which year did Brazil win the World Cup for the first time?

a) 1934

b) 1950

c) 1958

9 Who was the captain of Argentina's World Cup-winning team in 1986?

a) Jorge Burruchaga

b) Diego Maradona

c) Jorge Valdano

10 What tactical theory of play – pioneered by Netherlands coach Rinus Michels – came to prominence during the 1974 finals?

a) Total football

b) Sexy soccer

c) All out football

A

1	b
2	b
3	b
4	a
5	c
6	a
7	c
8	c
9	b
10	a

WORLD CUP – PART 2

1 Jack Taylor refereed the World Cup final in 1974. What was his occupation?

a) Butcher

b) Optician

c) Bank manager

2 Which player scored a record 13 goals in the 1958 tournament in Sweden?

a) Pele

b) Ferenc Puskas

c) Just Fontaine

3 What was unusual about the game between USA and Switzerland played in Detroit in 1994?

a) Played indoors

b) Delayed because of a power failure

c) Abandoned because of a thunderstorm

4 Who were the losing World Cup finalists in both 1934 and 1962?

a) France

b) Hungary

c) Czechoslovakia

5 Who was the leading scorer in the 1966 tournament in England?

a) Geoff Hurst

b) Eusebio

c) Florian Albert

6 **Which France player was sent off in the 1998 World Cup final against Brazil?**

a) Marcel Desailly

b) Zinedine Zidane

c) Frank Leboeuf

7 **During the opening ceremony of USA '94, which singer missed a strategically arranged penalty?**

a) Celine Dion

b) Madonna

c) Diana Ross

8 **France beat Brazil by a 3–0 margin in the 1998 final in Paris. Zinedine Zidane scored twice. Who scored the other goal?**

a) Emmanuel Petit

b) Lilian Thuram

c) Laurent Blanc

9 **Who was Argentina's successful chain-smoking manager when they were hosts of the tournament in 1978?**

a) Carlos Bilardo

b) César Luis Menotti

c) Omar Sivori

10 **When the USA beat England during the 1950 World Cup in Brazil, who scored the only goal of the game?**

a) Joe Gaetjens

b) Charlie Colombo

c) Ed Souza

A

1   a

2   c

3   a

4   c

5   b

6   a

7   c

8   a

9   b

10   a

WORLD CUP – PART 3

1 **Who was the captain of Brazil's World Cup-winning team in 2002?**

a) Ronaldo

b) Roberto Carlos

c) Cafu

2 **Which country held the first World Cup finals in Europe?**

a) Italy

b) England

c) Spain

3 **Which France player was sent off in the 2006 final played in Berlin?**

a) Laurent Blanc

b) Zinedine Zidane

c) Patrick Vieira

4 **In which year did Wales last qualify for the World Cup finals?**

a) 1958

b) 1974

c) 1982

5 **Which Romania star of the tournaments in 1990, 1994 and 1998 was known as the 'Maradona of the Carpathians'?**

a) Viorel Moldovan

b) Gheorghe Hagi

c) Florin Raducioiu

6 How old was Cameroon striker Roger Milla when he played in his third finals in 1994?

a) 39 years

b) 42 years

c) 45 years

7 In Spain in 1982, which Northern Ireland player became the youngest to appear in the World Cup finals?

a) John O'Neill

b) Felix Healy

c) Norman Whiteside

8 During which World Cup was a match decided by penalty shoot-out for the first time?

a) 1978

b) 1982

c) 1986

9 The World Cup trophy was stolen in London in 1966. What was the name of the dog that found it?

a) Pickles

b) Tickles

c) Biggles

10 The first World Cup was called the Jules Rimet Trophy. What position did he hold at FIFA from 1921–54?

a) General Secretary

b) Chair

c) President

A

1	c
2	a
3	b
4	a
5	b
6	b
7	c
8	b
9	a
10	c

GREAT IMPORTS

1 Along with Ossie Ardiles, which Argentina international joined Tottenham Hotspur in 1978?

a) Mario Kempes

b) Ricky Villa

c) Alberto Tarantini

2 From which club did Chelsea sign goalkeeper Petr Cech in 2004?

a) Stade Rennais

b) Sparta Prague

c) NEC Nijmegen

3 Thierry Henry joined Arsenal from which club in 1999?

a) Juventus

b) Barcelona

c) Monaco

4 Brothers George and Ted Robledo both played for Newcastle United in the 1952 FA Cup final. Where were they born?

a) Chile

b) Canada

c) Cyprus

5 Which German World Cup winner was signed by Liverpool in 1997?

a) Rudi Völler

b) Lothar Matthäus

c) Karl-Heinz Riedle

6 Chelsea signed Andriy Shevchenko for a British club record fee in 2006. What was the reported sum?

a) £25.1m

b) £30.8m

c) £35.5m

7 Which Denmark international was manager of Hull City in 2002?

a) Michael Laudrup

b) Jan Molby

c) Morten Olsen

8 Which England captain was born in Singapore?

a) Ron Flowers

b) David Platt

c) Terry Butcher

9 Which Middlesbrough forward was fondly known as 'the White Feather'?

a) Fabrizio Ravanelli

b) Juninho

c) Jan-Aage Fjortoft

10 Which First Division club did the Yugoslavia midfielder Vladimir Petrovic play for in the 1982–3 season?

a) West Bromwich Albion

b) Sunderland

c) Arsenal

A

1 b

2 a

3 a

4 a

5 c

6 b

7 b

8 c

9 a

10 c

FOOTBALL LEAGUE

1 Which national newspaper sponsored the Football League in the 1986–7 season?

a) *The Times*

b) *Today*

c) *Daily Mirror*

2 Who were the last champions of the Football League prior to the introduction of the Premier League in 1992?

a) Liverpool

b) Arsenal

c) Leeds United

3 Who was the secretary of the Football League from 1979 to 1989?

a) Alan Hardaker

b) Ted Croker

c) Graham Kelly

4 Which club plays home games at Oakwell Stadium?

a) Barnsley

b) Rotherham United

c) Chesterfield

5 In 1978, Wigan Athletic became the last club to be elected to the Football League. Who did they replace?

a) Barrow

b) Accrington Stanley

c) Southport

6 Prior to the introduction of the Premier League, which club won the Football League title on the most occasions?

a) Arsenal

b) Liverpool

c) Manchester United

7 Which player has scored the most goals in the history of the Football League, with a total of 434?

a) Arthur Rowley

b) Jimmy Greaves

c) Ian Rush

8 In which season was the three-points-for-a-win system introduced?

a) 1973–4

b) 1981–2

c) 1988–9

9 Which was the first season in the 20th century to include play-offs?

a) 1971–2

b) 1979–80

c) 1986–7

10 Which club did Alf Ramsey guide to the First Division title in 1962?

a) Tottenham Hotspur

b) Wolverhampton Wanderers

c) Ipswich Town

A

1 b

2 c

3 c

4 a

5 c

6 b

7 a

8 b

9 c

10 c

NON-LEAGUE

---

1 A national league outside of the Football League was created in 1979. What was it called?

a) National Conference

b) Alliance Premier League

c) Fifth Division

---

2 Who was the chief executive of the Football Conference from 1999 to 2007?

a) John Moules

b) Graham Kelly

c) Jim Thompson

---

3 In 1987, which club became the first to be automatically promoted from non-league to the Football League?

a) Wycombe Wanderers

b) Barnet

c) Scarborough

---

4 Which former Premier League boss became manager of Gainsborough Trinity in September 2009?

a) Ron Atkinson

b) Brian Little

c) Bobby Gould

---

5 Which club, owned by members of the MyFootballClub website since 2008, changed its name to Ebbsfleet United in 2007?

a) Fleet Town

b) Maidstone United

c) Gravesend & Northfleet

FOOTBALL

6 Which club played their home games at the Drill Field ground from 1875 to 2002?

a) Northwich Victoria

b) New Brighton

c) Glossop North End

7 In which year were Bishop's Stortford the last-ever winners of the FA Amateur Cup?

a) 1974

b) 1981

c) 1987

8 Which current Football League club won the FA Trophy in 1992?

a) Colchester United

b) Wycombe Wanderers

c) Yeovil Town

9 What was the original name of the regional league covering London and the south-east which, due to a sponsorship deal in 1997, has since been known as the Ryman League?

a) Hellenic League

b) Isthmian League

c) Southern League

10 Who was appointed manager of the England C national football team (then known as the England National Game XI) in January 2003?

a) John Owens

b) Paul Fairclough

c) Mick Wadsworth

A

1 b

2 a

3 c

4 b

5 c

6 a

7 a

8 a

9 b

10 b

23

SCOTTISH FOOTBALL

1   Who succeeded Jock Stein as manager of Celtic in 1978?

a)   David Hay

b)   Danny McGrain

c)   Billy McNeill

2   Which club are nicknamed 'the Gable Endies'?

a)   Montrose

b)   Queen's Park

c)   Raith Rovers

3   Prior to Aberdeen in 1979–80, who were the only club to break Celtic and Rangers' domination of the Scottish league title since 1962?

a)   Heart of Midlothian

b)   Kilmarnock

c)   Dundee United

4   Which was the first season of a four division format in Scottish league football?

a)   1975–6

b)   1987–8

c)   1994–5

5   Which club replaced Gretna in the Scottish Football League in 2008?

a)   Annan Athletic

b)   Spartans

c)   Peterhead

6 Which Scottish club reached the semi-final of the European Cup in 1983–4?

a) Aberdeen

b) Rangers

c) Dundee United

7 In the immediate postwar period, which Scottish club had a forward line that became fondly known as 'the Famous Five'?

a) Dundee

b) Hibernian

c) Motherwell

8 In 1885 Arbroath won a Scottish Cup tie 36–0, setting a British club record. Who were their opponents?

a) Vale of Leven

b) Renton

c) Bon Accord

9 In which town do Albion Rovers play their home games?

a) Coatbridge

b) Kirkcaldy

c) Dingwall

10 Which First Division club did Rangers face in the Scottish Cup final in 2008?

a) Queen of the South

b) Partick Thistle

c) St Johnstone

A

1	c
2	a
3	b
4	c
5	a
6	c
7	b
8	c
9	a
10	a

ENGLISH FOOTBALL TRIVIA

1 In which year were the first matches in the Football League played?

a) 1872

b) 1888

c) 1893

2 What was the name of the competition contested for four seasons from 1970 to 1973 by the highest scoring teams from each division of the Football League?

a) The Watney Cup

b) The Texaco Cup

c) The Rumbelows Cup

3 Which club has made the most appearances in the League Cup final?

a) Manchester United

b) Arsenal

c) Liverpool

4 Where did Bolton Wanderers play their home games before moving to the Reebok Stadium in 1997?

a) Burnden Park

b) Brunton Park

c) Borough Park

5 Which club did Mark Lawrenson manage from 1989 to 1990?

a) Oxford United

b) Norwich City

c) Tranmere Rovers

6 How many clubs in Devon were members of the Football League during the 2009–10 season?

a) One

b) Two

c) Three

7 Where became the new home of the Football Association headquarters in August 2009?

a) Wembley Stadium

b) Canary Wharf

c) Soho Square

8 As a player, with which club did Don Revie win an FA Cup winners' medal in 1956?

a) Huddersfield Town

b) Manchester City

c) Leicester City

9 Which club are nicknamed 'the Glovers'?

a) Carlisle United

b) Yeovil Town

c) Bradford City

10 Notts County are recognised as the oldest League club in the world. In which year were they formed?

a) 1862

b) 1874

c) 1880

A

1	b
2	a
3	c
4	a
5	a
6	c
7	a
8	b
9	b
10	a

ENGLAND TEAM

1 In which year did Fabio Capello score a winning goal for Italy against England at Wembley?

a) 1969

b) 1973

c) 1980

2 Which club was Peter Shilton playing for when he won the first of his 125 caps?

a) Leicester City

b) Stoke City

c) Nottingham Forest

3 Who holds the record with Bobby Moore of captaining England on 90 occasions?

a) David Beckham

b) Bryan Robson

c) Billy Wright

4 Who did Theo Walcott succeed as England's youngest-ever player in 2006?

a) Wayne Rooney

b) Michael Owen

c) Duncan Edwards

5 Which England centre-forward earned the nickname 'the Lion of Vienna' following a fine performance in Austria in 1952?

a) Tommy Lawton

b) Nat Lofthouse

c) Jackie Milburn

6 Who failed to convert the last penalty when England were eliminated from the 1998 World Cup in a shoot-out against Argentina?

a) Gareth Southgate

b) Paul Ince

c) David Batty

7 Who finished second behind England in their qualifying group for the World Cup in Japan and South Korea in 2002?

a) Germany

b) Poland

c) Greece

8 Who scored England's goal in their World Cup quarter-final win against Argentina in 1966?

a) Geoff Hurst

b) Bobby Charlton

c) Roger Hunt

9 During the 1966 World Cup finals, England faced France, Mexico and which other country at the group stage?

a) Switzerland

b) Chile

c) Uruguay

10 Who scored England's goal in their 1–0 World Cup 2006 win against Ecuador in Stuttgart?

a) Steven Gerrard

b) David Beckham

c) Frank Lampard

A

1	b
2	a
3	c
4	a
5	b
6	c
7	a
8	a
9	c
10	b

ENGLAND MANAGERS

1 With which club did Kevin Keegan begin his playing career?

a) Doncaster Rovers

b) Hartlepool United

c) Scunthorpe United

2 Which club did Sven Goran Eriksson lead to Italy's Serie A title in 1999–2000?

a) Lazio

b) Sampdoria

c) Internazionale

3 Apart from Ipswich Town, Sir Alf Ramsey was the manager of which Football League club?

a) Coventry City

b) Birmingham City

c) Leicester City

4 In which year did Terry Venables become England manager?

a) 1993

b) 1994

c) 1995

5 Who became England's caretaker manager in 1974 following the sacking of Sir Alf Ramsey?

a) Joe Mercer

b) Bill Nicholson

c) Dave Sexton

6 In how many World Cup finals tournaments did England compete with Walter Winterbottom as manager?

a) Two

b) Four

c) Six

7 With which club did Graham Taylor initially recommence his managerial career after leaving his post as England manager?

a) Aston Villa

b) Watford

c) Wolverhampton Wanderers

8 How many times did Bobby Robson play for England at full international level?

a) 6

b) 20

c) 53

9 Who replaced Fabio Capello as manager of Real Madrid in June 2007?

a) Vicente del Bosque

b) Guus Hiddink

c) Bernd Schuster

10 Along with which fellow England international did Glenn Hoddle join AS Monaco in 1987?

a) Mark Hateley

b) Ray Wilkins

c) Chris Waddle

A

1	c
2	a
3	b
4	b
5	a
6	b
7	c
8	b
9	c
10	a

WOMEN'S FOOTBALL

1 In which season was the Women's UEFA Champions League staged for the first time?

a) 1992–3

b) 2001–2

c) 2007–8

2 Who was appointed manager of England's Women's team in 1998?

a) Hope Powell

b) Rachel Yankey

c) Marianne Spacey

3 Including the 2009 tournament in Finland, how many consecutive Women's European Championships have Germany won?

a) Three

b) Five

c) Seven

4 Who stepped down as manager of the Arsenal Ladies team in 2009?

a) Eartha Pond

b) Clare Wheatley

c) Vic Akers

5 Which FA Women's Premier League team are known as 'the Belles'?

a) Millwall

b) Doncaster Rovers

c) Birmingham City

6 Apart from the USA and Germany, which is the only other nation to have won the Women's World Cup?

a) Norway

b) Italy

c) Australia

7 Who was England's captain at the 2009 European Championships in Finland?

a) Casey Stoney

b) Faye White

c) Sue Smith

8 When was the FA Women's Cup final staged for the first time?

a) 1963

b) 1971

c) 1984

9 Who was the leading scorer at the 2007 Women's World Cup finals in China?

a) Kelly Smith (England)

b) Birgit Prinz (Germany)

c) Marta (Brazil)

10 Who were the winners of the first Women's European Championships in 1984?

a) Scotland

b) Sweden

c) Yugoslavia

A

1	b
2	a
3	b
4	c
5	b
6	a
7	b
8	b
9	c
10	b

VENUES

1 What did the first FA Cup final at Wembley Stadium become known as?

a) White Horse final

b) Black Cat final

c) Brown Bear final

2 Which Portuguese team play their home games at Estadio da Luz?

a) FC Porto

b) Sporting Lisbon

c) Benfica

3 Where do Forfar Athletic play their home games?

a) Firhill

b) Station Park

c) McDiarmid Park

4 Which stadium staged the 2006 World Cup final?

a) Westfalenstadion, Dortmund

b) Allianz Arena, Munich

c) Olympiastadion, Berlin

5 Where was the first official international match in England played?

a) Kennington Oval

b) Crystal Palace

c) Stamford Bridge

FOOTBALL

6 **What was the name of Wigan Athletic's home ground before they moved to the JJB Stadium in 1999?**

a) Springhead Park

b) Springfield Park

c) Spring Road Park

7 **What is the name of the stadium built in Cape Town for the 2010 World Cup?**

a) Green Point Stadium

b) Red Spot Stadium

c) Yellow Peak Stadium

8 **Where was the first European Cup final staged in 1956?**

a) Stadio Olimpico, Rome

b) Parc des Princes, France

c) Santiago Bernabéu, Madrid

9 **Which Premier League ground's stands include the Trinity Road stand and Holte End?**

a) Anfield

b) White Hart Lane

c) Villa Park

10 **Prior to Scunthorpe United in 1988, which was the last Football League club to move to a new ground?**

a) Southend United

b) Port Vale

c) Hull City

A

1	a
2	c
3	b
4	c
5	a
6	b
7	a
8	b
9	c
10	a

REFEREES

1 Which referee awarded a record five penalties in the space of 27 minutes in a Second Division match between Crystal Palace and Brighton & Hove Albion in March 1989?

a) Mike Reed

b) Kelvin Morton

c) Trelford Mills

2 Which English referee is said to have come up with the idea for yellow and red cards during the World Cup tournament in 1966?

a) Jim Finney

b) George Courtney

c) Ken Aston

3 Following a successful career in football, which referee went on to work alongside Stuart Hall on the TV gameshow *It's a Knockout*?

a) Arthur Ellis

b) Jack Taylor

c) Clive Thomas

4 In 1994–5, who became the first female to be appointed on the list of Football League assistant referees?

a) Kim George

b) Pat Dunne

c) Wendy Toms

5 In 2008, Stuart Attwell became the youngest referee to officiate in the Premier League. In which year was he born?

a) 1978

b) 1982

c) 1986

FOOTBALL

6 **Who refereed the Champions League final in 1999, the World Cup final in 2002, and the UEFA Cup final in 2004?**

a) Pierluigi Collina

b) Lubos Michel

c) Horacio Elizondo

7 **Which FA Cup final referee later became president of FIFA?**

a) Charles Alcock

b) Stanley Rous

c) W. F. Bunnell

8 **In which year did linesmen officially become known as assistant referees?**

a) 1984

b) 1990

c) 1996

9 **Who preceded Mike Riley as general manager of the Professional Game Match Officials Board?**

a) Keith Hackett

b) Philip Don

c) David Elleray

10 **Who was the first referee to send a player off in an FA Cup final?**

a) Peter Willis

b) Peter Jones

c) Peter Walton

A

1	b
2	c
3	a
4	c
5	b
6	a
7	b
8	c
9	a
10	a

INTERNATIONAL ROUND-UP

1 Who replaced Joao Havelange as president of FIFA in 1998?

a) Franz Beckenbauer

b) Sepp Blatter

c) Jack Warner

2 Where are the World Cup finals due to be staged in 2014?

a) Brazil

b) Australia

c) Uruguay

3 What is the FIFA confederation in South America commonly known as?

a) CONCACAF

b) CAF

c) CONMEBOL

4 Which country won the football tournament at the Olympics in both 2004 and 2008?

a) Argentina

b) Spain

c) USA

5 Who was England's leading goal scorer during their successful qualifying campaign for the 2010 World Cup finals?

a) Peter Crouch

b) Wayne Rooney

c) Jermain Defoe

FOOTBALL

6 Who was appointed general secretary of UEFA in 2007?

a) David Taylor

b) Lars-Christer Olsson

c) Michel Platini

7 Which country has won the Africa Cup of Nations on the most occasions?

a) Cameroon

b) Nigeria

c) Egypt

8 When he retired in 2006, Mohamed Al-Deayea had set the record for the highest number of international appearances with 181 caps. Which country did he play for?

a) Saudi Arabia

b) Kuwait

c) United Arab Emirates

9 Who is the only person to have coached five different countries at five different World Cup finals?

a) Bora Milutinovic

b) Guus Hiddink

c) Philippe Troussier

10 What is the name of the tournament that features the champions of the six FIFA confederations and the World Cup holders and hosts?

a) FIFA Trophy

b) Confederations Cup

c) World Shield

A

1	b
2	a
3	c
4	a
5	b
6	a
7	c
8	a
9	a
10	b

39

CHAMPIONS LEAGUE

1 Which competition did the Champions League replace?

a) European Cup Winners' Cup

b) UEFA Super Cup

c) European Cup

2 In which season was the Champions League contested for the first time?

a) 1992–3

b) 1995–6

c) 1998–9

3 Who won the first Champions League Final?

a) AC Milan

b) Olympique de Marseille

c) Juventus

4 In the shoot-out at the end of the 2008 final, which Chelsea player took the last penalty (which was saved) to hand the Champions League trophy to Manchester United?

a) Nicolas Anelka

b) Frank Lampard

c) Juliano Belletti

5 Who became the first player to score 50 goals in the Champions League?

a) Ruud van Nistelrooy

b) Fernando Morientes

c) Raúl

6 **FC Unirea Urziceni qualified for the group stage of the Champions League for the first time in 2009. In which country is the club based?**

a) Bulgaria

b) Romania

c) Hungary

7 **Who is the first player to have won the Champions League with three different clubs?**

a) Thierry Henry

b) Hernán Crespo

c) Clarence Seedorf

8 **Which Turkish side did Liverpool beat 8–0 in 2007–8 to equal the record win under the new Champions League format?**

a) Fenerbahce

b) Trabzonspor

c) Besiktas

9 **Which Champions League record did Blackburn Rovers' Mike Newell set in December 1995?**

a) First hat-trick by a substitute

b) Quickest hat-trick

c) First hat-trick of penalties

10 **Which was the first team to win the Champions League when they were not their domestic league's current champions?**

a) Manchester United (1999)

b) Bayern Munich (2001)

c) Porto (2004)

A

1	c
2	a
3	b
4	a
5	c
6	b
7	c
8	c
9	b
10	a

EUROPEAN CHAMPIONSHIPS

1 Which Premier League player scored the winning goal in the Euro 2008 final in Vienna?

a) Michael Ballack

b) Cesc Fabregas

c) Fernando Torres

2 Which country won the 1992 tournament in Sweden after originally failing to qualify for the finals?

a) Croatia

b) Denmark

c) Russia

3 Up to and including 2008, which is the only country to have won the European Championship more than twice?

a) Germany

b) Italy

c) Spain

4 With a record nine goals, who was the leading scorer in the 1984 European Championship finals?

a) Michel Platini

b) Rudi Völler

c) Preben Elkjaer

5 Which country staged the first European Championship in 1960?

a) Italy

b) France

c) Germany

6 **Apart from Wembley, Old Trafford and Villa Park, which other ground staged a quarter-final at Euro 1996 in England?**

a) Anfield

b) Hillsborough

c) St James' Park

7 **Apart from co-hosts Austria, which was the only other country to be taking part in the European Championship finals for the first time in 2008?**

a) Poland

b) Slovenia

c) Turkey

8 **Who was the coach of Greece when they won Euro 2004 in Portugal?**

a) Karel Bruckner

b) Anghel Iordanescu

c) Otto Rehhagel

9 **Which two countries are co-hosting the Euro 2012 tournament?**

a) Croatia and Hungary

b) Sweden and Norway

c) Poland and Ukraine

10 **What was unusual about coach Raymond Domenech's TV interview shortly after France had been eliminated from Euro 2008?**

a) He announced his resignation

b) He proposed to his partner

c) He claimed he was planning to climb Everest

A

1	c
2	b
3	a
4	a
5	b
6	a
7	a
8	c
9	c
10	b

HALL OF FAME AND SHAME

1 Who was the first non-British or Irish winner of the Football Writers' Association Footballer of the Year award?

a) Bert Trautmann

b) Jürgen Klinsmann

c) Dennis Bergkamp

2 In 1999, Ken Richardson was found guilty of conspiring to burn down the main stand of which club?

a) Scarborough Athletic

b) Doncaster Rovers

c) Scunthorpe United

3 Who was the first British or Irish winner of the Ballon d'Or, the European Footballer of the Year award?

a) Stanley Matthews

b) Denis Law

c) George Best

4 Who was the first player to be sent off in an FA Cup final at Wembley?

a) Kevin Moran

b) Gordon McQueen

c) Paul McGrath

5 Who was the first player from an English club to win the FIFA World Player of the Year award?

a) Gary Lineker

b) Thierry Henry

c) Cristiano Ronaldo

6 Which Premier League player was banned for seven months after failing a drugs test in 2004?

a) Adrian Mutu

b) Edgar Davids

c) Jaap Stam

7 Which managerial duo were added to the National Football Museum's Hall of Fame in 2009?

a) George Allison and Tom Whittaker

b) Brian Clough and Peter Taylor

c) Joe Mercer and Malcolm Allison

8 Why was former Cardiff City striker Dai Thomas jailed for 60 days in 2002?

a) Involved in crowd trouble at a football match

b) Drink driving

c) Dealing in firearms

9 Which former England international received his knighthood in June 2004?

a) Bobby Robson

b) Trevor Brooking

c) Tom Finney

10 Sports agent Murdo Mackay was one of three men found guilty of defrauding which club in 2009?

a) Derby County

b) Nottingham Forest

c) Coventry City

A

1 a

2 b

3 a

4 a

5 c

6 a

7 c

8 a

9 b

10 a

STATISTICS

Which player has made the most full international appearances for each of the following countries?

1 Argentina
a) Javier Zanetti
b) Diego Maradona
c) Gabriel Batistuta

2 Brazil
a) Ronaldo
b) Claudio Taffarel
c) Cafu

3 Denmark
a) Morten Olson
b) Peter Schmeichel
c) Brian Laudrup

4 Germany
a) Jürgen Klinsmann
b) Lothar Matthäus
c) Per Mertesacker

5 Mexico
a) Claudio Suarez
b) Jared Borgetti
c) Hugo Sanchez

6 Holland
a) Ruud Gullit
b) Jaap Stam
c) Edwin van der Sar

7 Northern Ireland
a) Pat Jennings
b) David Healy
c) Nigel Worthington

8 Portugal
a) Eusebio
b) Luis Figo
c) Simao Sabrosa

9 Scotland
a) David Weir
b) Alan Rough
c) Kenny Dalglish

10 Wales
a) Neville Southall
b) Mark Hughes
c) Barry Horne

A

1 a

2 c

3 b

4 b

5 a

6 c

7 a

8 b

9 c

10 a

CRICKET

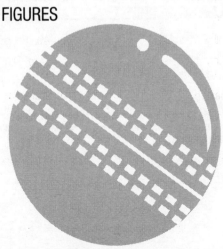

THE ASHES – PART 1

1 Since 1896, how many times have England beaten Australia in Test matches at Lord's?

a) Two

b) Four

c) Six

2 At which ground did England score their highest Ashes innings total of 903–7 (declared) in 1938?

a) Edgbaston

b) The Oval

c) Bramall Lane

3 With a total of 195, which bowler has taken the most wickets in Ashes history?

a) Shane Warne

b) Ian Botham

c) Hugh Trumble

4 Who was appointed England's captain for the first postwar series in Australia in 1946–7?

a) Wally Hammond

b) Bill Edrich

c) Bill Voce

5 Which of the following England players took the catch – off a Graeme Swann delivery – that clinched a crucial Ashes win at the Oval in 2009?

a) Paul Collingwood

b) Matt Prior

c) Alastair Cook

6   Which batsman has scored the most centuries for England in Ashes Tests?

a)   John Edrich

b)   David Gower

c)   Jack Hobbs

7   Who partnered Australia's Glenn McGrath in an unbroken last wicket stand to earn a draw in the third Test at Old Trafford in 2005?

a)   Matthew Hayden

b)   Damien Martyn

c)   Brett Lee

8   In what year did Jim Laker take a record 46 wickets in an Ashes series?

a)   1948

b)   1956

c)   1961

9   At which ground did Don Bradman hit his highest Ashes total of 33 in 1930?

a)   Headingley

b)   Lord's

c)   Trent Bridge

10 Who was captain when England regained the Ashes in Australia in 1970–1?

a)   Tony Greig

b)   Ray Illingworth

c)   Mike Denness

A

1	a
2	b
3	a
4	a
5	c
6	c
7	c
8	b
9	a
10	b

THE ASHES – PART 2

1 Which ground staged the first Ashes Test in December 1882?

a) Adelaide Oval

b) Melbourne Cricket Ground

c) WACA, Perth

2 Apart from Jonathan Trott, who was the only batsman to score a century for England in the 2009 series?

a) Paul Collingwood

b) Andrew Strauss

c) Ian Bell

3 Who is the only England bowler to take a hat-trick in an Ashes contest in England?

a) Fred Trueman

b) Jack Hearn

c) Andrew Flintoff

4 In 1882, which newspaper published the famous mock obituary announcing that the ashes of English cricket were being taken to Australia?

a) *The Sporting Times*

b) *The Guardian*

c) *Financial Times*

5 A legendary third Test victory at Headingley in 1981 was inspired by the performances of Ian Botham and Bob Willis. What was England's winning margin?

a) 18 runs

b) 52 runs

c) 1 wicket

CRICKET

6   Who was Australia's leading run scorer in the 2009 series in England?

a) Ricky Ponting

b) Simon Katich

c) Michael Clarke

7   During the 1974–5 series, which veteran England batsman was flown out to Australia following injuries inflicted by the bowling of Dennis Lillee and Jeff Thomson?

a) Colin Cowdrey

b) Tom Graveney

c) Ted Dexter

8   Who was Australia's captain during their first postwar tour of England in 1948?

a) Don Bradman

b) Sid Barnes

c) Ray Lindwall

9   Due to England's bowling tactics, the 1932–3 series in Australia became known by what name?

a) Streamline

b) Headline

c) Bodyline

10 Which batsman scored 173 not out, enabling England to get the 315 runs necessary to win the fourth Test at Leeds in 2001?

a) Mark Butcher

b) Nasser Hussain

c) Mark Ramprakash

A

1   b

2   b

3   b

4   a

5   a

6   c

7   a

8   a

9   c

10 a

COUNTY CRICKET

1 Which county's badge is described as a bear and ragged staff?

a) Yorkshire

b) Warwickshire

c) Somerset

2 Which Sussex player beat his own county record score with an innings of 344 against Somerset in August 2009?

a) Murray Goodwin

b) Michael Yardy

c) Luke Wright

3 Prior to Durham in 1992, which county most recently joined the County Championship?

a) Lancashire

b) Gloucestershire

c) Glamorgan

4 How many counties competed in the first official County Championship in 1890?

a) Four

b) Eight

c) Twelve

5 Who became the first sponsors of the County Championship in 1977?

a) Coca-Cola

b) Schweppes

c) Prudential

6 In which year was the County Championship split into two divisions?

a) 1992

b) 1996

c) 2000

7 Which county has won the County Championship on the most occasions?

a) Somerset

b) Yorkshire

c) Middlesex

8 Which county plays its home games at the St Lawrence Ground?

a) Kent

b) Worcestershire

c) Essex

9 Which county's colours are described as dark green and scarlet?

a) Leicestershire

b) Lancashire

c) Nottinghamshire

10 Which county did Pakistan batsman Zaheer Abbas play for between 1976 and 1981?

a) Derbyshire

b) Hampshire

c) Gloucestershire

A

1	b
2	a
3	c
4	b
5	b
6	c
7	b
8	a
9	a
10	c

WORLD CUP – PART 1

1 In the 1975 World Cup final won by West Indies, who scored 102 runs against Australia?

a) Roy Fredericks

b) Clive Lloyd

c) Keith Boyce

2 In a 2007 match against India at Port of Spain, which team became the first to concede 400 runs in a World Cup innings?

a) Bermuda

b) Zimbabwe

c) East Africa

3 Where will the World Cup be staged in 2015?

a) England and Wales

b) Pakistan and India

c) Australia and New Zealand

4 Who was England's captain when the competition was played outside England for the first time in 1987?

a) Mike Gatting

b) Bob Willis

c) Robin Smith

5 Who won the Man of the Tournament award by taking 26 wickets during the 2007 World Cup, held in the West Indies?

a) Lasith Malinga

b) Glenn McGrath

c) Shaun Pollock

6 Up to the end of the 2007 tournament, which batsman had scored the most runs in the history of the World Cup?

a) Viv Richards

b) Adam Gilchrist

c) Sachin Tendulkar

7 Which country reached the final qualifying stage of the World Cup for the first time in 2009?

a) Afghanistan

b) Argentina

c) Cayman Islands

8 Which South Africa batsman scored a new competition record of 188 not out against the United Arab Emirates in 1996?

a) Hansie Cronje

b) Gary Kirsten

c) Kepler Wessels

9 Who was Australia's captain during the World Cup tournament held in Australia and New Zealand in 1992?

a) Allan Border

b) Kim Hughes

c) Steve Waugh

10 In the first competition in 1975, how many overs were due to be bowled in each innings?

a) 40

b) 50

c) 60

A

1	b
2	a
3	c
4	a
5	b
6	c
7	a
8	b
9	a
10	c

WORLD CUP – PART 2

1 Which team did Sri Lanka dismiss for 36 runs during the 2003 World Cup?

a) Canada

b) Scotland

c) East Africa

2 Which South Africa batsman scored six sixes in an over during a World Cup game against the Netherlands in 2007?

a) Mark Boucher

b) Herschelle Gibbs

c) Andrew Hall

3 At the time of Bob Woolmer's death, during the 2007 World Cup in the West Indies, of which country was he the coach?

a) England

b) South Africa

c) Pakistan

4 Which new World Cup record did Canada batsman John Davison set in his innings against West Indies in 2003?

a) Fastest century

b) Slowest half century

c) First batsman given out for obstructing the field

5 Traditional white clothing and red cricket balls were last used in which World Cup tournament?

a) 1979

b) 1987

c) 1996

6 Who was the South Africa captain who misread the Duckworth Lewis rules, meaning that they tied with Sri Lanka and were eliminated from their home tournament in 2003?

a) Hansie Cronje

b) Shaun Pollock

c) Graeme Smith

7 In the 2007 tournament, officially, the last eight teams competed in which round?

a) Quarter-finals

b) Round of Eight

c) Super Eights

8 In the first World Cup tournament, which opener scored 36 not out in an entire innings?

a) Sunil Gavaskar

b) Chris Tavare

c) Rick McCosker

9 Who was Sri Lanka's captain when they won the 1996 World Cup in Pakistan?

a) Hashan Tillakaratne

b) Arjuna Ranatunga

c) Muttiah Muralitharan

10 In 2003, which non-Test playing nation became the first to reach a World Cup semi-final?

a) Ireland

b) Kenya

c) Namibia

A

1	a
2	b
3	c
4	a
5	b
6	b
7	c
8	a
9	b
10	b

GREAT IMPORTS

1 **For which country did former England coach Duncan Fletcher play international cricket?**

a) Australia

b) Zimbabwe

c) South Africa

2 **Apart from Somerset, which county did Viv Richards play for?**

a) Gloucestershire

b) Warwickshire

c) Glamorgan

3 **Where was England captain Tony Greig born?**

a) Queenstown, South Africa

b) Queensland, Australia

c) Queen's Park, Scotland

4 **Who was Yorkshire's first overseas player?**

a) Richie Richardson

b) Darren Lehmann

c) Sachin Tendulkar

5 **Which county did South Africa-born Kevin Pietersen join in 2000?**

a) Nottinghamshire

b) Hampshire

c) Middlesex

6 **For which English county did Australian fast bowler Jeff Thomson play during 1981?**

a) Lancashire

b) Somerset

c) Middlesex

7 **Which West Indies batsman scored 126 runs for Lancashire when they beat Warwickshire in the Gillette Cup final in 1972?**

a) Clive Lloyd

b) Alvin Kallicharran

c) Farokh Engineer

8 **Which overseas batsman hit an English first-class innings record of 501 not out in 1994?**

a) Mohammad Azharuddin

b) Brian Lara

c) Mark Waugh

9 **Which South Africa bowler joined Surrey as one of their overseas players in 2009?**

a) Shaun Pollock

b) Andre Nel

c) Makhaya Ntini

10 **Who was the first overseas player to win the Professional Cricketers' Association Player of the Year award on more than one occasion?**

a) Mike Procter

b) Andy Roberts

c) Waqar Younis

A

1	b
2	c
3	a
4	c
5	a
6	c
7	a
8	b
9	b
10	a

TEST CRICKET

1 Against England in April 2004, where did West Indies batsman Brian Lara score his world record 400 not out?

a) Barbados

b) Antigua

c) Jamaica

2 Who in 1999 went 101 minutes without scoring in a completed Test match innings?

a) Abdul Razzaq

b) Curtly Ambrose

c) Geoff Allott

3 Which Australian has scored the most runs in Test cricket?

a) Ricky Ponting

b) Steve Waugh

c) Allan Border

4 With whom did Mahela Jayawardene set a Test record partnership of 624 for Sri Lanka against South Africa in 2006?

a) Marvan Atapattu

b) Avishka Gunawardene

c) Kumar Sangakkara

5 In 2003, West Indies created a record by scoring 418 runs in the fourth innings to win a Test match. Who were their opponents?

a) Australia

b) Bangladesh

c) India

6 **Who was the first batsman to score 40 Test match centuries?**

a) Sachin Tendulkar

b) Geoff Boycott

c) Sunil Gavaskar

7 **Who was India's captain when they won their first Test in England in 1971?**

a) Nawab of Pataudi

b) Ajit Wadekar

c) Madan Lal

8 **Which Pakistan bowler took nine wickets in the match when they won in South Africa for the first time in 1998?**

a) Mushtaq Ahmed

b) Javed Miandad

c) Salman Butt

9 **Who became the first New Zealander to score 2,000 runs and take 200 wickets in Test cricket?**

a) Chris Cairns

b) Richard Hadlee

c) Nathan Astle

10 **Who became the first player to be out for a duck 40 times in his Test career?**

a) Chris Martin

b) Glenn McGrath

c) Courtney Walsh

A

1	b
2	c
3	a
4	c
5	a
6	a
7	b
8	a
9	b
10	c

ONE-DAY INTERNATIONALS

1   In which year did the first official One-Day International take place?

a)   1969

b)   1971

c)   1973

2   Who became the first England player to score 1,000 runs and take 100 wickets in a One-Day International career?

a)   Ian Botham

b)   Darren Gough

c)   Andrew Flintoff

3   Who was the first player to captain his country in over 200 One-Day Internationals?

a)   Mohammad Azharuddin (India)

b)   Imran Khan (Pakistan)

c)   Stephen Fleming (New Zealand)

4   In 2009, who became the first umpire to stand in his 200th One-Day International?

a)   Rudi Koertzen

b)   Daryl Harper

c)   Billy Bowden

5   Which Pakistan batsman set a new record of 37 balls for the fastest One-Day International 100 in 1996?

a)   Mohammad Yousuf

b)   Moin Khan

c)   Shahid Afridi

6 Who did South Africa replace at the top of the ICC World One-Day International rankings in January 2009?

a) Australia

b) India

c) New Zealand

7 In a One-Day International in 1981, with New Zealand needing six runs to tie the game with Australia, who bowled the last ball underarm and along the ground?

a) Ian Chappell

b) Greg Chappell

c) Trevor Chappell

8 Which country has England met most often in One-Day Internationals?

a) Australia

b) India

c) Sri Lanka

9 In January 2009 who became the oldest player – at 39 years and 212 days – to hit a One-Day International century?

a) Ricky Ponting

b) Sanath Jayasuriya

c) Mark Boucher

10 Which two venues in South Africa staged the ICC Champions Trophy in 2009?

a) Cape Town and Port Elizabeth

b) East London and Durban

c) Johannesburg and Centurion

A

1	b
2	a
3	c
4	a
5	c
6	a
7	c
8	a
9	b
10	c

INTERNATIONAL TWENTY20

1 In which year did the first Twenty20 international take place?

a) 2001

b) 2003

c) 2005

2 Where was the first Twenty20 World Cup staged in 2007?

a) South Africa

b) England

c) Pakistan

3 Which country won the first Twenty20 World Cup final?

a) Australia

b) India

c) Sri Lanka

4 In the Twenty20 World Cup, Sri Lanka became the first team to score more than 250 runs in an innings. Who were their opponents?

a) Kenya

b) West Indies

c) New Zealand

5 Which player scored the most runs in the 2009 Twenty20 World Cup in England?

a) Tillakaratne Dilshan

b) Jacob Oram

c) AB de Villiers

6 Which West Indies batsman became the first scorer of an international Twenty20 century during the 2007 World Cup?

a) Shivnarine Chanderpaul

b) Dwayne Smith

c) Chris Gayle

7 Which former South Africa Test batsman was India's coach during the 2009 Twenty20 World Cup?

a) Lance Klusener

b) Daryll Cullinan

c) Gary Kirsten

8 Who did Sri Lanka lose to in the final of the 2009 Twenty20 World Cup at Lord's?

a) West Indies

b) England

c) Pakistan

9 Which Australia bowler took the first hat-trick in an international Twenty20 innings against Bangladesh in 2007?

a) Brett Lee

b) Glenn McGrath

c) Andrew Symonds

10 Who captained England in their first Twenty20 international against Australia in 2005?

a) Michael Vaughan

b) Andrew Flintoff

c) Andrew Strauss

A

1	c
2	a
3	b
4	a
5	a
6	c
7	c
8	c
9	a
10	a

WOMEN'S CRICKET

1 Who was the captain of England's 2009 Women's World Cup winning team?

a) Claire Taylor

b) Beth Morgan

c) Charlotte Edwards

2 In which year was the Women's Cricket Association founded?

a) 1745

b) 1926

c) 1960

3 In 2004, who became the first woman to sit on the MCC general committee?

a) Rachael Heyhoe-Flint

b) Kate Hoey

c) Barbara Daniels

4 In which year was the Women's World Cup staged for the first time?

a) 1973

b) 1979

c) 1987

5 Which team won the Women's County Championship for the third time in four years in 2009?

a) Durham

b) Cornwall

c) Kent

6 Playing against West Indies in 2004, Pakistan's Kiran Baluch set a new record for the highest score in a Women's Test match innings. How many runs did she score?

a) 242

b) 365

c) 400

7 In 1998, who broke Rachael Heyhoe-Flint's record for the most runs in a Women's Test match career?

a) Clare Connor

b) Sandhya Agarwal

c) Janette Brittin

8 Where was the 2009 Women's World Cup held?

a) Australia

b) England

c) Pakistan

9 Who replaced Mark Dobson as head coach of the England Women's team in 2008?

a) Graham Ford

b) Karen Smithies

c) Mark Lane

10 Who did England beat in the 2009 Women's Twenty20 World Cup final?

a) Pakistan

b) New Zealand

c) West Indies

A

1	c
2	b
3	a
4	a
5	c
6	a
7	c
8	a
9	c
10	b

ALL-ROUNDERS

1 Which all-rounder was a leading player with the so-called Transvaal 'Mean Machine' of the 1980s?

a) Mike Procter

b) Peter Pollock

c) Clive Rice

2 For which English county did the West Indian all-rounder Garry Sobers play?

a) Nottinghamshire

b) Somerset

c) Derbyshire

3 Which New Zealand all-rounder retired from Test cricket in 2009?

a) Ross Taylor

b) Jacob Oram

c) Jesse Ryder

4 Which county did the legendary all-rounder Wally Hammond play for between 1920 and 1951?

a) Gloucestershire

b) Kent

c) Surrey

5 Which Pakistan all-rounder is popularly known as 'Boom Boom'?

a) Shahid Afridi

b) Wasim Akram

c) Majid Khan

6 Which of the following current England selectors did not achieve the Test double of 1,000 runs and 100 wickets?

a) Geoff Miller

b) Ashley Giles

c) James Whitaker

7 In 2008, which captain became the first player to score two half-centuries and take at least four wickets in each innings in a single Test match?

a) Anil Kumble

b) Daniel Vettori

c) Mahela Jayawardene

8 In which country was the late England all-rounder Ben Hollioake born?

a) Australia

b) Canada

c) South Africa

9 Who was the first player to pass the twin milestone in Test matches of 10,000 runs and 250 wickets?

a) Jacques Kallis

b) Ian Botham

c) Garry Sobers

10 Which Bangladesh cricketer reached the top of the ICC One-Day International all-rounder rankings during 2009?

a) Habibul Bashar

b) Mashrafe Mortaza

c) Shakib Al Hasan

A

1	c
2	a
3	b
4	a
5	a
6	c
7	b
8	a
9	a
10	c

BATSMEN

1 Which batsman created a record by playing in 105 One-Day International matches without being out for a duck?

a) Vic Marks

b) Kepler Wessels

c) Wasim Bari

2 Which batsman has scored the most first-class runs for Yorkshire?

a) Herbert Sutcliffe

b) Geoff Boycott

c) Len Hutton

3 Who was the first England player to score a century on his Test debut?

a) Pelham Warner

b) Peter May

c) W. G. Grace

4 Graeme Hick scored over 64,000 runs in his career. Which county did he play for?

a) Warwickshire

b) Gloucestershire

c) Worcestershire

5 On which ground did Garry Sobers become the first batsman to hit six sixes in a first-class over in 1968?

a) Sophia Gardens, Cardiff

b) Stradey Park, Llanelli

c) St Helen's, Swansea

6   **Sachin Tendulkar became the first batsman to reach 12,000 runs in Test cricket in 2008. When did he make his Test debut?**

a)   1989

b)   1993

c)   1998

7   **With whom did Peter May set an England Test record partnership of 411 against the West Indies in 1957?**

a)   Colin Cowdrey

b)   Bill Edrich

c)   Ted Dexter

8   **In the 1978 series against the West Indies, which Australian became the first batsman to wear a helmet in a Test?**

a)   Ian Chappell

b)   Rod Marsh

c)   Graham Yallop

9   **Which batsman scored a record 18 centuries in a season in 1947?**

a)   Don Bradman

b)   Denis Compton

c)   Tom Graveney

10 **In 1993, England's Graham Gooch was out to which unusual form of dismissal against Australia at Old Trafford?**

a)   Handled the ball

b)   Hit the ball twice

c)   Timed out

A

1	b
2	a
3	c
4	c
5	c
6	a
7	a
8	c
9	b
10	a

BOWLERS

1   What is the name of the delivery that, for a right-hand bowler and a right-hand batsman, will turn from the leg side to the off side?

a)   Arm ball

b)   Bouncer

c)   Leg break

2   Which West Indies bowler has taken the most wickets in a Test career?

a)   Michael Holding

b)   Curtly Ambrose

c)   Courtney Walsh

3   Which South Africa bowler took the first Test wicket after the country was re-admitted to international cricket in 1991?

a)   Eddie Barlow

b)   Richard Snell

c)   Lance Klusener

4   Which spin bowler is widely credited with inventing a delivery called a 'doosra'?

a)   Saqlain Mushtaq

b)   Derek Underwood

c)   Stuart MacGill

5   How many overs are individual bowlers usually restricted to in a 50-over one-day game?

a)   Eight

b)   Ten

c)   Twelve

6 After Jim Laker in 1956, who was the next bowler to take ten wickets in a Test innings?

a) Anil Kumble

b) Bob Massie

c) Imran Khan

7 What feat was achieved by England bowling duo Bill Voce and Gubby Allen against Australia in 1936?

a) Two bowlers operating unchanged in a completed Test innings

b) Two bowlers each taking a hat-trick in a Test match

c) Two bowlers scoring centuries when batting in the same Test innings

8 Which bowler has taken the most first-class wickets for Middlesex?

a) Fred Titmus

b) John Emburey

c) Angus Fraser

9 Which Pakistan bowler was nicknamed 'the Sultan of Swing'?

a) Waqar Younis

b) Wasim Akram

c) Imran Khan

10 Against Pakistan at the Oval in 2003, who became the first England bowler to take a hat-trick in a One-Day International?

a) Dominic Cork

b) Mark Ealham

c) Jimmy Anderson

A

1 c
2 c
3 b
4 a
5 b
6 a
7 a
8 a
9 b
10 c

RECORD-BREAKERS

1 Who broke the record for the most runs by a batsman in a single day's play in 1994?

a) Viv Richards

b) Matthew Hayden

c) Brian Lara

2 Which Australian batsman set a new record for the most sixes in a match when playing for Gloucestershire in 1995?

a) Andrew Symonds

b) Mark Waugh

c) Richie Richardson

3 Which wicketkeeper broke John Murray's record for the most dismissals in a first-class career?

a) Rod Marsh

b) Bob Taylor

c) Deryck Murray

4 Which player in February 2010 became the first to score a double century in a One-Day International?

a) Sachin Tendulkar

b) Jacques Kallis

c) Kumar Sangakkara

5 Which record did England bowler Sydney Barnes set in the 1913–14 tour of South Africa?

a) Oldest player in a Test match

b) Most wickets in a Test series

c) Most LBW dismissals in a Test innings

6 Which player holds the record for the most centuries in a first-class career?

a) Jack Hobbs

b) Sunil Gavaskar

c) Glenn Turner

7 Who was the first batsman to break Len Hutton's 1938 record of 364 runs in a Test innings?

a) Don Bradman

b) Graham Gooch

c) Garry Sobers

8 At 18 years and 149 days, who set the record as England's youngest Test player in 1949?

a) Brian Close

b) Godfrey Evans

c) Trevor Bailey

9 Against Glamorgan in 2002, Surrey's Alistair Brown set a new world record for highest innings in a limited-overs game. How many runs did he score?

a) 232

b) 268

c) 301

10 Which batsman holds the record for the most runs in Test cricket for England?

a) Graham Gooch

b) David Gower

c) Colin Cowdrey

A

1 c
2 a
3 b
4 a
5 b
6 a
7 c
8 a
9 b
10 a

FACTS AND FIGURES

1 Which former England Test bowler was admitted to the first-class umpires list in 2009?

a) Derek Pringle

b) Nick Cook

c) Norman Cowans

2 Which country plays Test matches with the West Indies for the Frank Worrell Trophy?

a) England

b) Australia

c) South Africa

3 Who was Durham's captain during the 2009 season?

a) Will Smith

b) Michael Di Venuto

c) Phil Mustard

4 Who was the first batsman to hit 100 sixes in his Test career?

a) Ian Botham

b) Gordon Greenidge

c) Adam Gilchrist

5 Before becoming Carnegie in 2008, what was Yorkshire's one-day team officially called?

a) Tykes

b) Yorkies

c) Phoenix

6 Over his Test career, what was Don Bradman's batting average?

a) 77.76

b) 88.85

c) 99.94

7 Who was the only England player to appear in the inaugural season of the Indian Premier League in 2008?

a) Owais Shah

b) Dimitri Mascarenhas

c) Luke Wright

8 What is an umpire signalling when he repeatedly taps one shoulder with the opposite hand?

a) Revoking last signal

b) Short run

c) Five penalty runs to batting team

9 Against which team in 2009 did Pakistan's Umar Gul become the first bowler to take five wickets in a Twenty20 international?

a) Sri Lanka

b) New Zealand

c) Ireland

10 Who was named chairman of the England and Wales Cricket Board in 2007?

a) Giles Clarke

b) David Morgan

c) Mike Soper

A

1	b
2	b
3	a
4	c
5	c
6	c
7	b
8	c
9	b
10	a

GROUNDS

1   Which ground occupies part of a former racecourse?

a)   County Ground, Derby

b)   County Ground, Northampton

c)   County Ground, Southampton

2   Who completed 20 years in his post as head groundsman at Lord's in 2008?

a)   Peter Marron

b)   Andy Fogarty

c)   Mick Hunt

3   In a World Series match between WSC Australia and WSC World XI in 1977, which ground staged the first cricket match under floodlights?

a)   Football Park, Adelaide

b)   VFL Park, Melbourne

c)   RAS Showground, Sydney

4   Where have Oxford University regularly played their home games since 1827?

a)   The Parks

b)   The Fields

c)   The Meadows

5   Which county championship ground became well known for the lime tree that stood within the boundary rope?

a)   Arundel

b)   Leicester

c)   Canterbury

6 Which recently built football stadium is situated on the site of a former county cricket ground?

a) Reebok Stadium (Bolton Wanderers)

b) KC Stadium (Hull City)

c) Stadium of Light (Sunderland)

7 In which South African city would you find the Kingsmead ground?

a) Pretoria

b) Cape Town

c) Durban

8 Which ground has a Kirkstall Lane End?

a) Headingley

b) Old Trafford

c) Grace Road

9 Which ground staged the first Twenty20 Finals Day in 2003?

a) The Oval

b) Trent Bridge

c) New Road

10 With an estimated aggregate of 465,000 watching an India v Pakistan Test match in 1999, which ground hosted the highest-recorded attendance at a cricket match?

a) Eden Gardens, Kolkata

b) Wankhede Stadium, Mumbai

c) Chidambaram Stadium, Chennai

A

1 a

2 c

3 b

4 a

5 c

6 b

7 c

8 a

9 b

10 a

FIRSTS

1 In which year was the first Test match played?

a) 1858

b) 1877

c) 1895

2 Who were Victoria's opponents when they became the first team to score 1,000 runs in a first-class innings in 1923?

a) Tasmania

b) Queensland

c) New South Wales

3 In 1972 which English batsman became the first player to score a century in a One-Day International?

a) Frank Hayes

b) Keith Fletcher

c) Dennis Amiss

4 Which former player, now a first-class umpire, took a wicket with his first ball in Test cricket?

a) Neil Mallender

b) Mark Benson

c) Richard Illingworth

5 In 1951 who became the first batsman to be dismissed in a Test match for obstructing the field?

a) Cyril Washbrook

b) Len Hutton

c) Peter May

CRICKET

6 **Which Zimbabwe player became the first bowler to take a hat-trick against England in a One-Day International?**

a) Eddo Brandes

b) Grant Flower

c) Henry Olonga

7 **In 2008 who became the first batsman to score more than 150 runs in a Twenty20 game in England?**

a) Graham Napier

b) Vikram Solanki

c) Mark Chilton

8 **In which year did Viv Richards become the first batsman to score 1,500 runs in a calendar year?**

a) 1972

b) 1976

c) 1980

9 **In 2008 which team won the title in the inaugural season of the Indian Premier League?**

a) Chennai Superkings

b) Rajasthan Royals

c) Delhi Daredevils

10 **Andrew Sandham was the first batsman to score a triple hundred in a Test match innings in 1930. For which county did he play?**

a) Worcestershire

b) Nottinghamshire

c) Surrey

A

1 b

2 a

3 c

4 c

5 b

6 a

7 a

8 b

9 b

10 c

 UMPIRES

Which county did the following umpires play for?

1   Dickie Bird
a)   Yorkshire
b)   Surrey
c)   Glamorgan

2   Barry Dudleston
a)   Lancashire
b)   Sussex
c)   Leicestershire

3   Mark Benson
a)   Nottinghamshire
b)   Kent
c)   Derbyshire

4   Ian Gould
a)   Northamptonshire
b)   Middlesex
c)   Warwickshire

5   John Holder
a)   Hampshire
b)   Sussex
c)   Surrey

6   Richard Illingworth
a)   Kent
b)   Yorkshire
c)   Worcestershire

7   Tim Robinson
a)   Nottinghamshire
b)   Northamptonshire
c)   Sussex

8   Peter Hartley
a)   Lancashire
b)   Yorkshire
c)   Durham

9   Nigel Llong
a)   Kent
b)   Middlesex
c)   Essex

10 David Shepherd
a)   Gloucestershire
b)   Glamorgan
c)   Somerset

A

1   a
2   c
3   b
4   b
5   a
6   c
7   a
8   b
9   a
10 a

RUGBY UNION

WORLD CUP

1 **Which World Cup marked the end of Keith Wood's Ireland international career?**

a) 1999

b) 2003

c) 2007

2 **Who was England's coach at the 2007 World Cup?**

a) Bill Beaumont

b) Andy Robinson

c) Brian Ashton

3 **Who was sacked as Wales coach after their defeat to Fiji in the 2007 tournament?**

a) Gareth Jenkins

b) Graham Henry

c) Allan Davies

4 **Which country won the first Rugby World Cup?**

a) South Africa

b) New Zealand

c) Australia

5 **Against which nation did New Zealand's Simon Culhane set a record in 1995 for the number of points in a World Cup match?**

a) Wales

b) Japan

c) Canada

6   Which player has scored the most points in the Rugby World Cup finals stage during his career?

a)   Jonny Wilkinson

b)   David Campese

c)   Andrew Mehrtens

7   Which Caribbean island hosted the first qualifying games for the 2011 World Cup?

a)   Grand Cayman

b)   Trinidad

c)   Barbados

8   Which country won the women's Rugby World Cup for the third time in 2006?

a)   USA

b)   New Zealand

c)   Australia

9   In which Rugby World Cup did South Africa make their first appearance?

a)   1991

b)   1995

c)   1999

10 Which country has been selected to host the 2015 World Cup?

a)   England

b)   Japan

c)   France

A

1	b
2	c
3	a
4	b
5	b
6	a
7	a
8	b
9	b
10	a

SIX NATIONS

1 **In which year did Croke Park first stage matches in the Six Nations?**

a) 2007

b) 2008

c) 2009

2 **How many bottles of champagne can the Six Nations trophy accommodate?**

a) Five

b) Six

c) Ten

3 **Against which team did Scotland score 12 tries in 1887, setting a record that still stands?**

a) England

b) Ireland

c) Wales

4 **Which England player in 2001 scored a record 89 points in a single Six Nations tournament?**

a) Jonny Wilkinson

b) Jeremy Guscott

c) Mike Catt

5 **Which countries tied for first place in the 1973 tournament?**

a) England and France

b) England, France and Scotland

c) All five competing nations

6 Which Scottish rugby union legend scored 288 points including 77 penalties in Six Nations games between 1986 and 1995?

a) Scott Hastings

b) John Jefferies

c) Gavin Hastings

7 Against which country did Ieuan Evans make his debut for Wales in February 1987?

a) France

b) England

c) Ireland

8 Which player scored a record 30 points for Ireland against Italy in 2000?

a) Keith Wood

b) Brian O'Driscoll

c) Ronan O'Gara

9 Who retired in 1996 having equalled C. N. Lowe's record of 18 tries for England in the tournament?

a) Rory Underwood

b) Jeremy Guscott

c) Rob Andrew

10 Diego Dominguez won 74 caps for Italy, but how many appearances did he make for his native Argentina?

a) None

b) Two

c) Seven

A

1	a
2	a
3	c
4	a
5	c
6	c
7	a
8	c
9	a
10	b

TEST MATCHES

1 Who scored the first try in a rugby union Test at the Stade de France?

a) Gavin Henson

b) Austin Healey

c) Philippe Bernat-Salles

2 Who provided the opposition when Wales played their first Test match at the Millennium Stadium?

a) England

b) South Africa

c) New Zealand

3 What nationality is rugby union referee Alain Rolland?

a) Irish

b) French

c) South African

4 Who succeeded Bernard Laporte as head coach of France in October 2007?

a) Serge Blanco

b) Jean-Pierre Rives

c) Marc Lièvremont

5 In which year did Argentina announce their arrival as a rugby union force by winning their first match against Australia?

a) 1979

b) 1982

c) 1985

6 Who was head coach of the British and Irish Lions for their 2005 tour of New Zealand?

a) Clive Woodward

b) Ian McGeechan

c) Bill Beaumont

7 In 1939, which southern hemisphere side returned home without playing a game after arriving in England the day before war was declared?

a) South Africa

b) New Zealand

c) Australia

8 Which was the first major southern hemisphere side to be beaten by Ireland?

a) Australia

b) Argentina

c) South Africa

9 Which venue in 1923 hosted Scotland's last home match against England before the opening of Murrayfield?

a) Raeburn Place

b) Inverleith

c) Hampden Park

10 Which country in 1910 hosted the first official tour by a combined British Isles rugby union team?

a) South Africa

b) Australia

c) Canada

A

1	c
2	b
3	a
4	c
5	a
6	a
7	c
8	a
9	b
10	a

DOMESTIC GAME

1 Which player followed a successful rugby league career with Wigan by playing union for Saracens and England?

a) Andy Farrell

b) Brian Carney

c) Martin Johnson

2 Which English club was punished after a player feigned injury in the 'Bloodgate' affair?

a) Harlequins

b) Leeds

c) Wasps

3 Which team won the first John Player Special Cup in 1972?

a) Northampton

b) Bath

c) Gloucester

4 In which season were play-offs first used to decide the English Premiership champions?

a) 2002–3

b) 2003–4

c) 2004–5

5 How many teams comprise the RFU Championship, introduced in the 2009–10 season?

a) 12

b) 16

c) 18

6   Which club was the first to win the Scottish Championship and the Scottish Cup?

a)   Hawick

b)   Gala

c)   Melrose

7   Which rugby league side won the Middlesex Sevens in 1996?

a)   Hull Kingston Rovers

b)   Wigan Warriors

c)   Bradford Bulls

8   How many English teams competed in the first Heineken Cup in 1995–6?

a)   None

b)   Two

c)   Four

9   After which famous player is the County Championship Cup now named?

a)   Bill Beaumont

b)   Jeremy Guscott

c)   Will Carling

10 Which club was the first to win the Celtic League?

a)   Glasgow

b)   Leinster

c)   Munster

A

1	a
2	a
3	c
4	a
5	a
6	a
7	b
8	a
9	a
10	b

GREAT PLAYERS

1 Which legend of Welsh rugby retired in 1972 at the age of only 27?

a) Gareth Edwards

b) J. P. R. Williams

c) Barry John

2 Philippe St Andre turned his back on a career in which sport to commit to rugby union?

a) Rugby league

b) Tennis

c) Swimming

3 Who made his Wales debut against Japan in 2001 and was voted IRB Young Player of the Year in the same year?

a) Rob Jones

b) Shane Williams

c) Gavin Henson

4 Against which minor rugby nation did Chris Paterson make his Scotland debut in 1999?

a) Spain

b) Portugal

c) Iceland

5 Which player represented Australia 101 times before retiring in 1999?

a) Michael Lynagh

b) David Campese

c) Tim Horan

6 **Who captained the British and Irish Lions on their unbeaten tour of South Africa in 1974?**

a) Willie John McBride

b) Gareth Edwards

c) Fergus Slattery

7 **In which South American country was French rugby legend Serge Blanco born?**

a) Chile

b) Argentina

c) Venezuela

8 **Who became the youngest player to be capped for the All Blacks when he made his debut against France in 1994?**

a) Jonah Lomu

b) Christian Cullen

c) Doug Howlett

9 **Which South African player scored eight tries in the 2007 World Cup, equalling the tournament record?**

a) Bryan Habana

b) Percy Montgomery

c) Francois Steyn

10 **Who did Martin Johnson succeed as England captain in 1999?**

a) Richard Hill

b) Phil de Glanville

c) Lawrence Dallaglio

A

1 c

2 b

3 c

4 a

5 b

6 a

7 c

8 a

9 a

10 c

HIGHS AND LOWS

1 Which team set a record in 1994 by scoring 164 points in a match against Singapore?

a) New Zealand

b) Japan

c) Hong Kong

2 In June 1998, which team inflicted England's heaviest defeat of 76–0?

a) Australia

b) South Africa

c) New Zealand

3 Against which team did Scotland's Gavin Hastings score a record 44 points at the 1995 World Cup?

a) Namibia

b) Ivory Coast

c) Portugal

4 Which nation beat Wales in the 2007 World Cup group stage to prevent them from reaching the quarter-finals?

a) Samoa

b) Japan

c) Fiji

5 Which English player was the first in the world to score more than 2,000 points in official IRB Sevens internationals?

a) Joe Rokocoko

b) William Ryder

c) Ben Gollings

6 Which nation was the first to have a player sent off in a Rugby World Cup finals match?

a) Romania

b) Tonga

c) Wales

7 Who is the most capped player in international rugby?

a) Jason Leonard

b) George Gregan

c) Sean Fitzpatrick

8 Which Lions captain led the 1974 tour of South Africa, in which the third Test erupted into a brawl as the tourists reacted to strong-arm Springbok tactics?

a) Phil Bennett

b) Willie John McBride

c) Gordon Brown

9 As at 2010, who holds the record for the number of points scored by a player in the Six Nations tournament?

a) Ronan O'Gara

b) Jonny Wilkinson

c) Neil Jenkins

10 After the Five Nations tournament began in 1910, which team was the first to lose all its matches in one tournament?

a) Scotland

b) France

c) Wales

A

1   c

2   a

3   b

4   c

5   c

6   c

7   b

8   b

9   b

10   b

TWICKENHAM

1 What was the ground on which Twickenham stadium was built previously used for?

a) Grazing cattle

b) Playing cricket

c) Growing cabbages

2 Who did England play in the first international at the stadium in 1910?

a) Wales

b) South Africa

c) Barbarians

3 Which now annual fixture took place at Twickenham for the first time in 1921?

a) The Varsity match

b) The Calcutta Cup

c) The Combined Services match

4 What was Cyril Brownlie the first player to do at Twickenham in 1925?

a) Score a hat-trick of tries

b) Catch a streaker

c) Be sent off

5 In which year did England and South Africa play the first floodlit match at Twickenham?

a) 1987

b) 1991

c) 1995

6 Which touring side did England beat for the first time when they visited Twickenham in December 1969?

a) Australia

b) Argentina

c) South Africa

7 In which year did Erica Roe streak across the Twickenham pitch?

a) 1977

b) 1982

c) 1987

8 Who did England play when Twickenham hosted the Rugby World Cup final in 1991?

a) Australia

b) New Zealand

c) South Africa

9 In which year did Twickenham host its first Sunday match in the Six Nations championship?

a) 2003

b) 2006

c) 2009

10 Which member of the royal family opened the new East Stand in 1994?

a) The Queen

b) Prince Charles

c) Princess Anne

A

1 c

2 a

3 a

4 c

5 c

6 c

7 b

8 a

9 a

10 a

HISTORY OF THE GAME

In which years did the following rugby union events occur?

1 Formation of Guy's Hospital Rugby Club?

a) 1843

b) 1888

c) 1912

2 First rugby match in New Zealand?

a) 1870

b) 1910

c) 1925

3 First Rugby World Cup?

a) 1985

b) 1987

c) 1991

4 Formation of the International Rugby Board?

a) 1886

b) 1905

c) 1932

5 Formation of the Women's Rugby Football Union?

a) 1983

b) 1988

c) 1993

6 First live TV broadcast of an international rugby match?

a) 1932

b) 1938

c) 1948

7 Introduction of the Mandela Plate for matches between South Africa and Australia?

a) 1990

b) 1995

c) 2000

8 Value of a drop goal reduced from four points to three?

a) 1948

b) 1953

c) 1958

9 The All Blacks earned the name 'the Invincibles'?

a) 1920

b) 1925

c) 1935

10 Value of a try increased to five points?

a) 1980

b) 1985

c) 1992

A

1 a

2 a

3 b

4 a

5 a

6 b

7 c

8 a

9 b

10 c

GOLF

THE MAJORS

1   Which is the first major of the year?

a)   US Open

b)   Masters

c)   PGA Championship

2   In which year did Tiger Woods win his first major?

a)   1995

b)   1996

c)   1997

3   Who was the first player from outside the USA to win the Masters?

a)   Bernhard Langer

b)   Seve Ballesteros

c)   Gary Player

4   At the start of the 2010 season, who held the record for most wins in majors?

a)   Jack Nicklaus

b)   Tiger Woods

c)   Ben Hogan

5   What nationality is Yang Yong-eun, first Asian winner of a major in 2009?

a)   Thai

b)   South Korean

c)   Taiwanese

6 Which big-hitter only qualified for the 1991 PGA Championship as ninth reserve yet went on to win the title?

a) Ian Woosnam

b) Paul Azinger

c) John Daly

7 Which was the last of the majors to become established?

a) Masters

b) US Open

c) PGA Championship

8 Who won the Masters in 2000?

a) Nick Faldo

b) Padraig Harrington

c) Vijay Singh

9 How many times did British golfers win the US Open before the first American success?

a) 12

b) 16

c) 25

10 What colour jacket is awarded to the winner of the Masters?

a) Green

b) Claret

c) Yellow

A

1	b
2	c
3	c
4	a
5	b
6	c
7	a
8	c
9	b
10	a

THE OPEN CHAMPIONSHIP

---

1 Which course staged the Open on the first 12 occasions that it was contested?

a) Muirfield

b) St Andrews

c) Prestwick

---

2 How many times did Seve Ballesteros win the Open?

a) Once

b) Three times

c) Five times

---

3 Which course hosted the Open in 1951, the only occasion it has been played outside England and Scotland?

a) Royal Dublin

b) Royal Portrush

c) Royal Belfast

---

4 Which course has hosted the Open more times than any other?

a) Prestwick

b) Royal Troon

c) St Andrews

---

5 What was the winner's prize at the first Open in 1860?

a) Claret Jug

b) Challenge Belt

c) Golden Putter

6 How many years elapsed between Gary Player's first and last victories in the Open?

a) Seven

b) Twelve

c) Fifteen

7 Who won the Open in 1951, the last British golfer to win prior to Tony Jacklin's victory in 1969?

a) Dick Burton

b) Max Faulkner

c) Henry Cotton

8 What is the official name of the Claret Jug?

a) Open Trophy

b) British Open Trophy

c) Golf Champion Trophy

9 In which year did Tiger Woods win the Open for the first time?

a) 2000

b) 2003

c) 2005

10 What achievement at the Open is commemorated by a silver medal, first awarded in 1949?

a) Leading amateur

b) Hole in one

c) Longest drive

A

1	c
2	b
3	b
4	c
5	b
6	c
7	b
8	c
9	a
10	a

THE RYDER CUP

1 Which course is due to stage the Ryder Cup in 2014?

a) Augusta

b) Gleneagles

c) Wentworth

2 How many points are at stake in each Ryder Cup tournament?

a) 18

b) 24

c) 28

3 Who was the first player from outside the British Isles to captain the European team?

a) Bernhard Langer

b) Seve Ballesteros

c) José María Olazábal

4 How many times did Great Britain win the Ryder Cup prior to the addition of players from Europe?

a) Three

b) Five

c) Eight

5 Who ended a run of three European victories when he captained the USA to success in 2008?

a) Paul Azinger

b) Curtis Strange

c) Corey Pavin

6 Which player did Samuel Ryder immortalise by placing his likeness on top of the trophy?

a) Ted Ray

b) George Duncan

c) Abe Mitchell

7 When was the Ryder Cup opened to players from continental Europe?

a) 1975

b) 1979

c) 1983

8 Which player in 1967 completed a hat-trick of wins as captain, 20 years after first leading his team to victory?

a) Jerry Barber

b) Ben Hogan

c) Sam Snead

9 In 1929 which Yorkshire golf club became the first to host the Ryder Cup in England?

a) Moortown

b) Ganton

c) Lindrick

10 Who succeeded Tony Jacklin as captain of the European team for the 1991 tournament?

a) Bernard Gallacher

b) Sam Torrance

c) Mark James

A

1	b
2	c
3	b
4	a
5	a
6	c
7	b
8	b
9	a
10	a

RECORDS

1 Who finished the year in top spot when the official world rankings were introduced in 1986?

a) Jack Nicklaus

b) Seve Ballesteros

c) Greg Norman

2 Which player has spent the most weeks at the top of the rankings?

a) Tiger Woods

b) Lee Trevino

c) Nick Faldo

3 Who in 1990 became the oldest US Open champion aged 45 years and 15 days?

a) Hale Irwin

b) Tom Kite

c) Fuzzy Zoeller

4 Which player has made the most Ryder Cup appearances with the European team?

a) Seve Ballesteros

b) Ian Woosnam

c) Nick Faldo

5 Who was the first European to win the PGA Championship after the event changed from match play to stroke play in 1958?

a) Tony Jacklin

b) Padraig Harrington

c) Sandy Lyle

6 Who staged a record final-round comeback of seven strokes to win the US Open in 1960?

a) Billy Casper

b) Bob Charles

c) Arnold Palmer

7 Who in 1999 equalled the record for the worst round carded by an Open Champion?

a) Ernie Els

b) Nick Price

c) Paul Lawrie

8 At which course in 1973 did Peter Butler record the first hole-in-one in the history of the Ryder Cup?

a) Wentworth

b) Muirfield

c) The Belfry

9 Who won the last of his record six Masters titles in 1986?

a) Ray Floyd

b) Jack Nicklaus

c) Tom Watson

10 What was unique about Densmore Shute's Open victory in 1933?

a) Same score in all four rounds

b) Biggest range of scores

c) Featured a hole-in-one

A

1	c
2	a
3	a
4	c
5	b
6	c
7	c
8	b
9	b
10	a

FAMOUS COURSES AND HOLES

At which of the world's great golf courses would you find the following famous features?

1 Hell Bunker

a) Royal Birkdale

b) St Andrews

c) Gleneagles

2 Punch Bowl

a) Royal Lytham & St Annes

b) Royal Liverpool

c) Musselburgh

3 Amen Corner

a) Bethpage State Park

b) Augusta

c) Brookline

4 Duel in the Sun

a) Prestwick

b) Royal Troon

c) Turnberry

5 The Maiden

a) Royal St Georges

b) Carnoustie

c) The Belfry

6 The Postage Stamp

a) Royal Birkdale

b) Royal Troon

c) Royal St Georges

7 The Brabazon Course

a) Wentworth

b) The Belfry

c) Turnberry

8 Murder Mile

a) Royal Lytham & St Annes

b) Gleneagles

c) Wentworth

9 Odin's Revenge

a) Oakland Hills

b) Valhalla

c) Augusta

10 The Barry Burn

a) The Belfry

b) Celtic Manor

c) Carnoustie

A

1 b

2 b

3 b

4 c

5 a

6 b

7 b

8 a

9 b

10 c

TENNIS

GRAND SLAMS

1 Which player in 1988 achieved a Golden Slam (all four Grand Slam events plus Olympic Gold)?

a) Boris Becker

b) Stefan Edberg

c) Steffi Graf

2 Including her triumphs in both singles and doubles, how many Grand Slam trophies did Martina Navratilova win?

a) 39

b) 49

c) 59

3 Which was the only Grand Slam event that Pete Sampras failed to win during his career?

a) US Open

b) French Open ·

c) Australian Open

4 Which player won the men's Grand Slam (all four events) twice in the 1960s?

a) Rod Laver

b) Ken Rosewall

c) Fred Stolle

5 What was the nickname of Maureen Connolly Brinker, the first women's Grand Slam winner in 1953?

a) Magic Mo

b) Mighty Mo

c) Little Mo

6   **Which venue hosted the US Open from 1915 until it moved to Flushing Meadow in 1978?**

a)   Los Angeles Tennis Center

b)   Newport Casino

c)   Forest Hills

7   **Which player denied Roger Federer a Grand Slam by winning the French Open in 2006 and 2007?**

a)   Albert Costa

b)   Rafael Nadal

c)   Marat Safin

8   **Prior to Virginia Wade, who was the last British player to win a Grand Slam singles event?**

a)   Fred Perry

b)   Sue Barker

c)   Ann Jones

9   **Which was the only Grand Slam event to continue during the Second World War?**

a)   French Open

b)   US Open

c)   Australian Open

10 **Mats Wilander won three out of four Grand Slam events in 1988. In which event did he miss out?**

a)   Wimbledon

b)   Australian Open

c)   French Open

A

1	c
2	c
3	b
4	a
5	c
6	c
7	b
8	b
9	b
10	a

WIMBLEDON

1 **Who did Virginia Wade beat to win the women's singles final in 1977?**

a) Evonne Cawley

b) Betty Stove

c) Olga Morozova

2 **What feature of the championships was introduced in 1927?**

a) Seeding

b) Wild cards

c) White clothing

3 **In 1905 which nation provided Wimbledon's first overseas champion, in the women's singles?**

a) USA

b) France

c) Australia

4 **What change was made at Wimbledon in 1971?**

a) The tie-break was introduced

b) Yellow balls were first used

c) Floodlights were introduced

5 **Who beat Charlie Pasarell in the 1969 match that lasted more than five hours and took 112 games to complete?**

a) Arthur Ashe

b) Ken Rosewall

c) Pancho Gonzales

6 **Which was the last of the other Grand Slam tournaments to abandon the use of grass courts?**

a) Australian Open

b) French Open

c) US Open

7 **Which former men's singles champion joined Tim Henman in an exhibition match to demonstrate the new roof over centre court in May 2009?**

a) Pete Sampras

b) Andre Agassi

c) Goran Ivanisevic

8 **Goran Ivanisevic, the first wild card to win Wimbledon, beat which player in the 2001 men's final?**

a) Pat Rafter

b) Pete Sampras

c) Tim Henman

9 **Who was the first unseeded player to win the men's singles?**

a) Michael Stich

b) Boris Becker

c) Pat Cash

10 **In which year did Wimbledon become an open event for amateur and professional players?**

a) 1965

b) 1968

c) 1972

A

1 b

2 a

3 a

4 a

5 c

6 a

7 b

8 a

9 b

10 b

DAVIS CUP

1 At which American university was the Davis Cup conceived?

a) Yale

b) Harvard

c) Princeton

2 Which countries set the record for the most games needed to decide a Davis Cup tie, with 327 in 1974?

a) India and Australia

b) Australia and New Zealand

c) Great Britain and Romania

3 Which country was runner-up in 1981, 2006 and 2008, but has never won the cup?

a) Croatia

b) Argentina

c) Switzerland

4 Which country beat Great Britain in 2009 to relegate them to Europe/Africa Zone Group II?

a) Netherlands

b) Iceland

c) Poland

5 Which country in 2005 became the first unseeded nation to win the cup?

a) Croatia

b) Russia

c) Belgium

TENNIS

6 **Which country refused to play the 1974 final as a protest against apartheid, handing South Africa a walkover victory?**

a) Australia

b) USA

c) India

7 **Who won Great Britain's only rubber the last time they contested the final, the 4–1 defeat against the USA in 1978?**

a) David Lloyd

b) Mark Cox

c) Buster Mottram

8 **What is the name of the women's equivalent of the Davis Cup?**

a) Fed Cup

b) Wightman Cup

c) Hopman Cup

9 **Who won all three of his matches in the final when Italy lifted the cup for the only time in 1976?**

a) Paolo Bertolucci

b) Adriano Panatta

c) Antonio Zugarelli

10 **In which decade did Great Britain last win the Davis Cup?**

a) 1930s

b) 1950s

c) 1960s

A

1	b
2	a
3	b
4	c
5	a
6	c
7	c
8	a
9	b
10	a

LINE CALLS AND FAULTS

1 **Which volatile tennis champion coined the catchphrase 'you cannot be serious'?**

a) Goran Ivanisevic

b) Jimmy Connors

c) John McEnroe

---

2 **Which top player reportedly broke a total of 48 rackets during 1999?**

a) Marat Safin

b) Greg Rusedski

c) Andre Agassi

---

3 **Which American player was banned for two grand slam tournaments after abusing the umpire and walking out of a match at Wimbledon in 1995?**

a) Jeff Tarango

b) Jim Courier

c) Michael Chang

---

4 **Which player was serving for the match in a US Open 2001 quarter-final against Lleyton Hewitt when he launched into a tantrum, called the umpire an 'absolute moron', received a warning and went on to lose his concentration and the match?**

a) Andy Roddick

b) Tim Henman

c) Pat Rafter

---

5 **After how many code violations does a player forfeit the match?**

a) Three

b) Four

c) Five

6 Which player became known as 'the Bucharest Buffoon' for on-court antics which included sinking to his knees to argue with the electronic line-call system?

a) Ilie Nastase

b) Ion Tiriac

c) Alex Radulescu

7 Which former women's number one followed up an argument with the umpire in the final of the 1999 French Open by delivering two underarm serves against Steffi Graf?

a) Monica Seles

b) Martina Hingis

c) Arantxa Sanchez Vicario

8 Who was disqualified from Wimbledon in 1995 after lashing out in frustration and accidentally hitting a ball girl with a ball?

a) Tim Henman

b) Jeremy Bates

c) Greg Rusedski

9 Which piece of tennis equipment was invented by a former aircraft engineer called Bill Carlton?

a) Hawkeye

b) Umpires' hydraulic chair

c) Cyclops

10 Who became so frustrated at the 2008 Miami Masters that he hit himself three times with his racket and needed treatment for a head wound?

a) Dmitry Tursunov

b) Yevgeny Kafelnikov

c) Mikhail Youzhny

A

1 c

2 a

3 a

4 a

5 b

6 a

7 b

8 a

9 c

10 c

DOUBLES

Who partnered the following to Wimbledon doubles success?

1 Michael Stich, 1992

a) Jimmy Connors

b) John McEnroe

c) Ilie Nastase

2 Mark Woodforde, 1993–7

a) Mats Wilander

b) Todd Woodbridge

c) Pat Cash

3 Steffi Graf, 1988

a) Gabriela Sabatini

b) Helena Sukova

c) Jo Durie

4 Venus Williams, various

a) Serena Williams

b) Lindsay Davenport

c) Kim Clijsters

5 Bob Bryan, 2006

a) Jamie Murray

b) Michael Llodra

c) Mike Bryan

6 Martina Navratilova, 1981–4

a) Kathy Jordan

b) Pam Shriver

c) Jana Novotna

7 Wendy Turnbull, 1983 and 1984

a) David Lloyd

b) John Lloyd

c) Buster Mottram

8 John Austin, 1980

a) Tracy Austin

b) Chris Evert

c) Billie Jean King

9 Jelena Jankovic, 2006

a) Jamie Murray

b) Arnaud Clement

c) Tim·Henman

10 Rosie Casals, 1968

a) Margaret Court

b) Billie Jean King

c) Betty Stove

A

1 b

2 b

3 a

4 a

5 c

6 b

7 b

8 a

9 a

10 b

HORSE RACING

CLASSICS

1 Which is the oldest of the Classic races?

a) The Derby

b) The St Leger

c) The Oaks

2 Which jockey recorded the last of his nine Derby wins on Teenoso in 1983?

a) Willie Carson

b) Lester Piggott

c) Joe Mercer

3 What was unique about Tontine's victory in the 1,000 Guineas in 1825?

a) She was the only entry

b) All the other horses fell

c) She finished third, but the first two horses were disqualified

4 Which racecourse hosted the St Leger when subsidence forced the race to be moved from Doncaster in 1989?

a) Ayr

b) York

c) Newmarket

5 Which horse won the fillies' version of the Triple Crown by winning the 1,000 Guineas, the Oaks and the St Leger in 1985?

a) Diomed

b) Oh So Sharp

c) Ile de Bourbon

6 **What is the name of the course used at Newmarket for the 1,000 and 2,000 Guineas?**

a) The Rowley Mile

b) The Guineas Mile

c) The Classic Mile

7 **Which Classic race was the scene of a suffragette protest in 1913, when Emily Davison ran out in front of the king's horse and subsequently died of her injuries?**

a) The Oaks

b) The Derby

c) The 2,000 Guineas

8 **With a distance of one mile and six furlongs, which Classic race is the longest?**

a) The Derby

b) The St Leger

c) The 1,000 Guineas

9 **At which Classic racecourse would you find Tattenham Corner?**

a) Epsom Downs

b) Doncaster

c) Sandown Park

10 **Which trainer's Derby winners included Slip Anchor, Reference Point and Oath?**

a) Aidan O'Brien

b) Michael Stoute

c) Henry Cecil

A

1	b
2	b
3	a
4	a
5	b
6	a
7	b
8	b
9	a
10	c

GRAND NATIONAL

1 **In which city is Aintree racecourse?**

a) Manchester

b) Liverpool

c) Chester

2 **What was the rather apt name of the winner of the first Grand National in 1839?**

a) Lottery

b) Jumper

c) First Past the Post

3 **How many runners made up the biggest field for a Grand National in 1929?**

a) 44

b) 55

c) 66

4 **Which is the last of the named fences to be jumped in the race?**

a) Foinavon

b) The Chair

c) Valentine's Brook

5 **Which horse won the 1992 Grand National as the country prepared for the general election?**

a) Downing Street

b) Party Politics

c) Major Minister

6 In which year did Red Rum win the first of his three Grand Nationals?

a) 1973

b) 1974

c) 1975

7 In 1982 Geraldine Rees became the first woman to complete the Grand National. What was the name of her horse?

a) Bucks Fizz

b) Bottoms Up

c) Cheers

8 Which jockey, who became a TV pundit, led over the last fence on Carrickbeg in the 1963 Grand National but lost the race by three-quarters of a length?

a) Lord Oaksey

b) Brough Scott

c) John McCririck

9 Who was the first woman to train a Grand National winner?

a) Venetia Williams

b) Lucinda Russell

c) Jenny Pitman

10 How many of the 16 fences on the course are jumped twice?

a) 10

b) 12

c) 14

A

1 b

2 a

3 c

4 c

5 b

6 a

7 c

8 a

9 c

10 c

INTERNATIONAL MEETINGS

1 Which racecourse is the home of the Irish National Hunt Festival?

a) Leopardstown

b) Galway

c) Punchestown

2 Which race meeting is recognised as the richest in the world?

a) Dubai World Cup

b) Breeders' Cup

c) Prix de l'Arc de Triomphe

3 Which American jockey won the first running of the Japan Cup in 1981?

a) Steve Cauthen

b) Cash Asmussen

c) Jerry Bailey

4 Which racecourse hosts the Kentucky Derby?

a) Churchill Downs

b) Belmont Park

c) Santa Anita

5 Which trainer saddled Dubai World Cup winners for Frankie Dettori, Richard Hills and Jerry Bailey?

a) Bob Baffert

b) Saeed bin Suroor

c) Michael Stoute

6 **Which Caribbean island is home to the Garrison Savannah racecourse?**

a) Antigua

b) Jamaica

c) Barbados

7 **Which jockey's four wins in the Prix de l'Arc de Triomphe include three in a row from 1985 to 1987?**

a) Yves Saint-Martin

b) Freddy Head

c) Pat Eddery

8 **Which Irish venue hosts a world-renowned racing festival for seven days every July?**

a) Galway

b) Naas

c) Wexford

9 **Which event is billed as 'the race that stops a nation'?**

a) The Kentucky Derby

b) The Arlington Million

c) The Melbourne Cup

10 **Which jockey achieved his first Classic success in Europe aboard Temporal in the German Derby in 1991?**

a) Frankie Dettori

b) Michael Kinane

c) Kieren Fallon

A

1	c
2	a
3	b
4	a
5	b
6	c
7	c
8	a
9	c
10	a

THE FLAT

1 What is the maximum distance for a sprint race?

a) Five furlongs

b) Six furlongs

c) Seven furlongs

2 Which course traditionally hosts the last major fixture of the Flat racing season?

a) Doncaster

b) Leicester

c) Newmarket

3 Which Group One race was established at Sandown in 1886 and is named after an undefeated 18th-century racehorse?

a) The Lockinge Stakes

b) The Eclipse Stakes

c) The Sussex Stakes

4 Which festival features seven of the 32 Group One races in a British Flat season?

a) The Ebor Festival

b) The Guineas Festival

c) Royal Ascot

5 Who won the title of British Flat Racing Champion Jockey a record 26 times?

a) Lester Piggott

b) Gordon Richards

c) Nat Flatman

6 Which racecourse counts the Nassau Stakes among its Group One fixtures?

a) Goodwood

b) Newbury

c) Cartmel

7 Which Flat jockey became the first woman to ride 100 winners in a calendar year?

a) Lisa Jones

b) Alex Greaves

c) Hayley Turner

8 Which is the only all-Flat racecourse in Scotland?

a) Kelso

b) Musselburgh

c) Hamilton Park

9 Who became British Flat Racing Champion Trainer for the first time in 1996?

a) Saeed bin Suroor

b) Mark Johnston

c) Aidan O'Brien

10 Starting stalls are now used in all Flat races, but in which year were they introduced?

a) 1965

b) 1970

c) 1975

A

1	c
2	a
3	b
4	c
5	b
6	a
7	c
8	c
9	a
10	a

NATIONAL HUNT

1   Which trainer saddled the first five horses home in the 1983 Cheltenham Gold Cup?

a)   David Nicholson

b)   Jenny Pitman

c)   Michael Dickinson

2   Which term is used to describe a National Hunt Flat race?

a)   Trotter

b)   Bouncer

c)   Bumper

3   Which horse made history in 1934 by winning the Grand National and the Cheltenham Gold Cup in the same season?

a)   Golden Miller

b)   Reynoldstown

c)   Royal Mail

4   Which jockey rode Best Mate to victory in three successive Cheltenham Gold Cups between 2002 and 2004?

a)   Mark Pitman

b)   Jim Culloty

c)   Adrian Maguire

5   In which year was the Cheltenham Festival among the many racing events cancelled because of foot-and-mouth disease?

a)   2000

b)   2001

c)   2002

6 **What is the name of the popular form of amateur National Hunt racing?**

a) Open hurdling

b) Cross-country

c) Point-to-point

7 **Which racecourse is the venue for the Midlands Grand National?**

a) Huntingdon

b) Leicester

c) Uttoxeter

8 **Which horse won the Grand National in 2006, the year after success in the Irish National?**

a) Hedgehunter

b) Numbersixvalverde

c) Monty's Pass

9 **Which trainer won the King George VI Chase three years running with Kauto Star from 2006 to 2008?**

a) Willie Mullins

b) Tom Taaffe

c) Paul Nicholls

10 In which year did the Welsh National move to its current home of Chepstow?

a) 1949

b) 1954

c) 1959

A

1　c

2　c

3　a

4　b

5　b

6　c

7　c

8　b

9　c

10　a

HORSES

1 Which horse was retired in October 2009 shortly after adding the Prix de l'Arc de Triomphe to wins in the 2,000 Guineas and the Derby?

a) Fame and Glory

b) Cavalryman

c) Sea the Stars

2 Which Triple Crown winner sired the Derby winners Golden Fleece, Lammtarra and Shahrastani?

a) Ile de Bourbon

b) Nijinsky

c) Mill Reef

3 Which famous grey retired in 1991 after a career that included four wins in the King George VI Chase?

a) The Fellow

b) Desert Orchid

c) Wayward Lad

4 Which Irish horse won the Cheltenham Gold Cup three years running in the 1960s?

a) Arkle

b) Mill House

c) What a Myth

5 Which horse won the Prix de l'Arc de Triomphe in 1977 and again in 1978?

a) Alleged

b) Rheingold

c) Dancing Brave

6 Which Derby winner was kidnapped from the Ballymany Stud in Ireland by masked gunmen in 1983?

a) Shergar

b) Troy

c) Shirley Heights

7 Which racehorse is buried beside the winning post at Aintree?

a) Red Rum

b) L'Escargot

c) Arkle

8 Which horse won the Champion Hurdle under Jonjo O'Neill and John Francome, and also enjoyed success on the Flat, winning the Chester Cup twice and the Ebor Handicap?

a) Night Nurse

b) Dawn Run

c) Sea Pigeon

9 Which horse lost the 2,000 Guineas to Brigadier Gerard in 1971, but bounced back to win the Derby and the Prix de l'Arc de Triomphe later that season?

a) Sassafras

b) Mill Reef

c) Roberto

10 Which horse went more than 100 races without a win and was described by the *Racing Post* as 'a seriously slow maiden in danger of becoming a folk hero'?

a) Quixall Crossett

b) Flockton Grey

c) Rapid Lad

A

1 c

2 b

3 b

4 a

5 a

6 a

7 a

8 c

9 b

10 a

 **COURSES**

1 Which racecourse is the home of the Scottish Grand National?

a) Perth

b) Ayr

c) Hamilton Park

2 At which course did Frankie Dettori win all seven races on the card in September 1996?

a) Ascot

b) Sandown Park

c) Kempton

3 Which is the most southerly racecourse in Great Britain?

a) Newton Abbot

b) Brighton

c) Goodwood

4 Which racecourse hosted the first Breeders' Cup meeting in 1984?

a) Churchill Downs

b) Belmont Park

c) Hollywood Park

5 Which course is home to the Prix de l'Arc de Triomphe?

a) Chantilly

b) Longchamp

c) Saint-Cloud

6 Which racecourse is the home of a festival known as 'Glorious'?

a) Goodwood

b) Newmarket

c) Chepstow

7 The name of which Irish racecourse is said to mean 'place of the running horse'?

a) The Curragh

b) Leopardstown

c) Thurles

8 At which racecourse would you find the July Course?

a) Market Rasen

b) Newbury

c) Newmarket

9 Which racecourse held its first meeting in June 2009?

a) Southwell

b) Great Leighs

c) Ffos Las

10 Which was the first course in Great Britain to offer floodlit racing?

a) Wolverhampton

b) Kempton Park

c) Aintree

A

1	b
2	a
3	a
4	c
5	b
6	a
7	a
8	c
9	c
10	a

HORSE RACING

JOCKEYS

1 Who was the champion National Hunt jockey three times before retiring with a neck injury in 1999?

a) Jonjo O'Neill

b) Phil Tuck

c) Richard Dunwoody

2 Which jockey was the first to ride 100 winners as a teenager in a British Flat racing season?

a) Lester Piggott

b) Frankie Dettori

c) Steve Cauthen

3 Which jockey built a new career as a bestselling crime writer following his retirement in 1957?

a) Aubrey Brabazon

b) Fred Winter

c) Dick Francis

4 Which jockey rode his 3,000th winner at Plumpton in February 2009?

a) Richard Johnson

b) Mick Fitzgerald

c) Tony McCoy

5 Which actor played the part of the jockey Bob Champion in the 1984 film *Champions*?

a) John Hurt

b) Donald Sutherland

c) Bob Hoskins

6 **At which racecourse did Frankie Dettori ride his first winner in Britain in June 1987?**

a) Beverley

b) Sandown

c) Goodwood

7 **Which famous jockey rode his only Derby winner in 1953, by which time he was 49 years old?**

a) Gordon Richards

b) Scobie Breasley

c) Geoff Lewis

8 **Who in 1997 became the first woman to ride the winner of a Group One race?**

a) Joanna Badger

b) Alex Greaves

c) Princess Anne

9 **At which French racecourse did Kieren Fallon fail a test for a banned substance in August 2007?**

a) Longchamp

b) Deauville

c) Chantilly

10 **Which jockey was a team captain on the BBC TV quiz show *A Question of Sport*?**

a) Willie Carson

b) Steve Cauthen

c) Walter Swinburn

A

1	c
2	a
3	c
4	c
5	a
6	c
7	a
8	b
9	b
10	a

TRAINERS

1 What was the first name of 'Ginger' McCain, who trained Red Rum to three Grand National victories?

a) Donald

b) Gerry

c) Danny

2 Who trained Lammtarra to win the Derby, the King George VI and Queen Elizabeth Diamond Stakes and the Prix de l'Arc de Triomphe in his first season with the Godolphin stable?

a) John Oxx

b) Luca Cumani

c) Saeed bin Suroor

3 Which trainer won three successive Cheltenham Gold Cups from 2007 to 2009 to add to his success in 1999?

a) Paul Nicholls

b) Noel Chance

c) Toby Balding

4 Who trained Dunfermline to win the St Leger for the Queen in 1977?

a) John Dunlop

b) Dick Hern

c) Michael Stoute

5 Which trainer saddled the winner of the 2009 Grand National?

a) Venetia Williams

b) Ann Duffield

c) Henrietta Knight

6 **Who was the champion trainer of National Hunt racing in 1993–4 and 1994–5, interrupting Martin Pipe's run of 15 titles?**

a) Robert Alner

b) David Elsworth

c) David Nicholson

7 **Which trainer achieved a record five wins in the Cheltenham Champion Hurdle when he saddled Sea Pigeon to win the race in 1980 and 1981?**

a) Paddy Mullins

b) Peter Easterby

c) Michael Stoute

8 **Which Irish trainer saddled the legendary Arkle?**

a) Tom Dreaper

b) Mick O'Toole

c) Charlie Mallon

9 **Who trained Nijinsky to win the Triple Crown of the 2,000 Guineas, the Derby and the St Leger in 1970?**

a) Henry Cecil

b) Vincent O'Brien

c) Ian Balding

10 **Which trainer won the Grand National in 1965 and 1966 having already won the race twice as a jockey?**

a) Pat Taaffe

b) Fred Winter

c) Tim Forster

A

1	a
2	c
3	a
4	b
5	a
6	c
7	b
8	a
9	b
10	b

THE DERBY

With which horse did the following jockeys and trainers achieve their first win in the Derby?

1 Lester Piggott
a) Nijinsky
b) Crepello
c) Never Say Die

2 Willie Carson
a) Troy
b) Henbit
c) Nashwan

3 Pat Eddery
a) Grundy
b) Golden Fleece
c) Quest for Fame

4 Kieren Fallon
a) Kris Kin
b) Oath
c) High Chaparral

5 Frankie Dettori
a) Benny the Dip
b) Motivator
c) Authorized

6 Michael Stoute
a) Shergar
b) Shahrastani
c) Teenoso

7 Henry Cecil
a) Slip Anchor
b) Oh So Sharp
c) Dr Devious

8 Aidan O'Brien
a) Lammtarra
b) Galileo
c) Sir Percy

9 Vincent O'Brien
a) Sir Ivor
b) St Paddy
c) Larkspur

10 John Oxx
a) Sinndar
b) Sea the Stars
c) Erhaab

A

1 c
2 a
3 a
4 b
5 c
6 a
7 a
8 b
9 c
10 a

BOXING

GREAT BRITONS

1 Which regal title was assumed by the Sheffield-born boxer Naseem Hamed?

a) Duke

b) King

c) Prince

2 The father of which champion boxer used to sing 'Danny Boy' before his fights?

a) Chris Finnegan

b) Barry McGuigan

c) Herol Graham

3 Which undefeated light welterweight champion of the world served as a Royal Marine and then worked as a firefighter before making his name as a boxer?

a) Terry Allen

b) Terry Marsh

c) Clinton McKenzie

4 Which British middleweight won two world title fights against Vito Antuofermo before losing to Marvin Hagler?

a) Alan Minter

b) Kevin Finnegan

c) Tony Sibson

5 Which Scot lost his world lightweight title in a controversial fight against Roberto Duran at Madison Square Garden in 1972?

a) Ken Buchanan

b) Jim Watt

c) Walter McGowan

6 Which nickname is shared by Manchester's Ricky Hatton and the American fighter Thomas Hearns?

a) Hero

b) Hardcase

c) Hitman

7 Which boxer famous for wearing jodhpurs, a bowler hat and a monocle was voted Britain's best-dressed man in 1991 and 1993?

a) Chris Eubank

b) Nigel Benn

c) Dave 'Boy' Green

8 Who became BBC Sports Personality of the Year in 2007 and retired undefeated in 2009?

a) Kevin McIntyre

b) Tony Oakey

c) Joe Calzaghe

9 At which Olympics did Amir Khan win a silver medal?

a) Sydney, 2000

b) Athens, 2004

c) Beijing, 2008

10 Which British fighter beat the world welterweight champion Donald Curry in six rounds in 1986, after Curry dismissed him as a 'ragamuffin'?

a) John H. Stracey

b) John Conteh

c) Lloyd Honeyghan

A

1 c

2 b

3 b

4 a

5 a

6 c

7 a

8 c

9 b

10 c

FAMOUS HEAVYWEIGHTS

1   Who was the only world heavyweight champion to retire with a perfect winning record?

a)   Jersey Joe Walcott

b)   Joe Louis

c)   Rocky Marciano

2   Which heavyweight won three successive Olympic gold medals in 1972, 1976 and 1980?

a)   Teofilo Stevenson

b)   George Foreman

c)   Henry Tillman

3   Who won eight successive British heavyweight titles from 1959 to 1967, regaining the title in 1970?

a)   Henry Cooper

b)   Brian London

c)   Jack Bodell

4   When did Cassius Clay change his name to Muhammad Ali?

a)   1962

b)   1964

c)   1966

5   Who won Olympic heavyweight gold in 1984 and became WBC heavyweight champion four years later?

a)   Bob Foster

b)   Joe Frazier

c)   Ken Norton

6   Which WBC champion beat IBF champion Tony Tucker to become undisputed world heavyweight champion in 1987?

a)   Mike Tyson

b)   James 'Bonecrusher' Smith

c)   Tim Witherspoon

7   Against which fighter did Sonny Liston win his first world heavyweight title in 1962?

a)   Ingemar Johansson

b)   Ernie Terrell

c)   Floyd Patterson

8   Who in 1993 became the first British fighter to win a world heavyweight title since 1897?

a)   Herbie Hide

b)   Frank Bruno

c)   Lennox Lewis

9   What is the nationality of Vitali and Wladimir Klitschko?

a)   Russian

b)   Ukrainian

c)   Polish

10   Which world heavyweight champion was also a proficient golfer and became the first African American to play a PGA Tour event?

a)   Joe Louis

b)   Ezzard Charles

c)   Jack Johnson

A

1	c
2	a
3	a
4	b
5	b
6	a
7	c
8	c
9	b
10	c

WORLD CHAMPIONS

1 At which weight did Sugar Ray Robinson win the world title five times?

a) Heavyweight

b) Light heavyweight

c) Middleweight

2 Which Irish boxer won world title fights against Chris Eubank and Nigel Benn?

a) Barry McGuigan

b) Steve Collins

c) Charlie Nash

3 What nationality is Anita Christensen, the former WBA women's bantamweight world champion?

a) British

b) Danish

c) Norwegian

4 Which Liverpool-born fighter was WBC light heavyweight champion from 1974–7?

a) Bunny Johnson

b) Chris Finnegan

c) John Conteh

5 Which boxer beat Thomas Hearns at Caesars Palace in 1981 to unify the world welterweight titles?

a) Sugar Ray Leonard

b) Marvin Hagler

c) Roberto Duran

6 Oscar De La Hoya became only the third man to win world titles in five different weight divisions, but who beat him in 2007 to become the fourth fighter to achieve the feat?

a) Floyd Mayweather Junior

b) Diego Corrales

c) Juan Manuel Marquez

7 Which football stadium was the venue for the world light welterweight title fight in 2008 between Ricky Hatton and Juan Lazcano?

a) Old Trafford

b) City of Manchester Stadium

c) Anfield

8 Who was a world champion at middleweight, super middleweight and light heavyweight before beating John Ruiz in 2003 to win the WBA heavyweight title?

a) Jeff Lacy

b) Felix Trinidad

c) Roy Jones Junior

9 Who became the youngest winner of a world heavyweight title when he beat Trevor Berbick in 1986?

a) Tony Tucker

b) Leon Spinks

c) Mike Tyson

10 In which class does British boxer Carl Froch compete?

a) Middleweight

b) Super middleweight

c) Heavyweight

1	c
2	b
3	b
4	c
5	a
6	a
7	b
8	c
9	c
10	b

 **BIG FIGHTS**

BOXING

Who did the following fighters beat to win world heavyweight title fights?

1 James J. Corbett, 1892

a) John L. Sullivan

b) Bob Fitzsimmons

c) Jack Root

2 Jack Dempsey, 1919

a) Jess Willard

b) Tommy Burns

c) Georges Carpentier

3 Joe Louis, 1947

a) Ezzard Charles

b) Johnny Paychek

c) Jersey Joe Walcott

4 Rocky Marciano, 1952

a) Jersey Joe Walcott

b) Joey Maxim

c) Brian London

5 Cassius Clay, 1964

a) Henry Cooper

b) Floyd Patterson

c) Sonny Liston

6 Joe Frazier, 1971

a) Henry Cooper

b) Muhammad Ali

c) Ken Norton

7 George Foreman, 1974

a) Joe Bugner

b) Joe Frazier

c) Ken Norton

8 Muhammad Ali, 1974

a) George Foreman

b) Joe Bugner

c) Richard Dunne

9 Frank Bruno, 1995

a) Riddick Bowe

b) Mike Tyson

c) Oliver McCall

10 Lennox Lewis, 2002

a) Mike Tyson

b) Frank Bruno

c) Evander Holyfield

A

1 a

2 a

3 c

4 a

5 c

6 b

7 c

8 a

9 c

10 a

OLYMPICS

Q GOLD MEDALLISTS

1   Which eastern European nation won water polo gold at three consecutive Olympics from 2000 to 2008?

a)   Romania

b)   Czech Republic

c)   Hungary

2   Who won boxing gold for Canada in the super-heavyweight division at the 1988 Olympics?

a)   Lennox Lewis

b)   Raymond Downey

c)   Tom Glesby

3   Michael Phelps swam to eight gold medals in Beijing 2008, but how many did he win in Athens 2004?

a)   None

b)   Six

c)   Eight

4   In which events did Larissa Latynina win nine gold medals between 1956 and 1964?

a)   Swimming

b)   Middle-distance running

c)   Gymnastics

5   What was the nickname of Ian Thorpe, the Australian swimmer who won five Olympic gold medals?

a)   The Shark

b)   Flipper

c)   Thorpedo

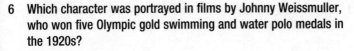

6 **Which character was portrayed in films by Johnny Weissmuller, who won five Olympic gold swimming and water polo medals in the 1920s?**

a) Tarzan

b) The Man from Atlantis

c) Captain Nemo

7 **In which field event did Al Oerter dominate for the USA, winning four consecutive gold medals from 1956 to 1968?**

a) Shot put

b) Javelin

c) Discus

8 **What nationality is Lasse Viren, winner of gold medals in the 5,000m and 10,000m in both Munich 1972 and Montreal 1976?**

a) Finnish

b) Czech

c) Hungarian

9 **Who was the first British competitor to win three gold medals in a single Games since 1908?**

a) Steve Redgrave

b) Bradley Wiggins

c) Chris Hoy

10 **Hungary's Aladar Gerevich holds the record for the most Olympic gold medals won in the same event. Which event is it?**

a) Sabre fencing

b) Pistol shooting

c) Archery

A

1 c

2 a

3 b

4 c

5 c

6 a

7 c

8 a

9 c

10 a

OLYMPICS

RECORD-BREAKERS

1 How many swimming world records were set at the 2008 Beijing Games?

a) 25

b) 50

c) 75

2 In which event at Beijing 2008 was a new women's world record set at 5.05m?

a) High jump

b) Shot put

c) Pole vault

3 Abhinav Bindra won a first individual gold medal for which country at the 2008 Beijing Games?

a) India

b) Sri Lanka

c) Singapore

4 To whom did the 100m world record broken by Usain Bolt at the 2008 Beijing Olympics belong?

a) Justin Gatlin

b) Usain Bolt

c) Tim Montgomery

5 In which event did Jackie Joyner-Kersee set a world record at the 1988 Olympics in Seoul?

a) Long jump

b) Heptathlon

c) Triple jump

6 Swimmers from which country set world records in the men's 4 x 100m and 4 x 200m freestyle relays at Sydney 2000?

a) Australia

b) South Africa

c) USA

---

7 Who was the only British athlete to set a world record at the 1968 Olympics in Mexico?

a) John Sherwood

b) David Hemery

c) Lillian Board

---

8 How many world records did the American swimmer Mark Spitz set at the Munich Games in 1972?

a) Five

b) Seven

c) Ten

---

9 What nationality is Alberto Juantorena, who set a world record in the 800m at the Montreal Olympics in 1976?

a) Jamaican

b) Spanish

c) Cuban

---

10 In which sport did Nurcan Taylan set two world records at Athens 2004, becoming the first woman to win Olympic gold for Turkey?

a) Weightlifting

b) Gymnastics

c) Cycling

A

1	a
2	a
3	a
4	b
5	b
6	a
7	b
8	b
9	c
10	a

TOP BRITS

1 Who was the first British woman to win gold in the Olympic 400m?

a) Christine Ohuruogu

b) Dame Kelly Holmes

c) Kathy Cook

2 Which Olympic gold medallist is the chairman of the organising committee for the London Games?

a) Sir Steve Redgrave

b) Daley Thompson

c) Lord Coe

3 Allan Wells won gold for Great Britain in the men's 100m in Moscow in 1980, but which medal did he pick up for the 200m?

a) Gold

b) Silver

c) Bronze

4 Which film told the story of Harold Abrahams and Eric Liddell at the 1924 Olympics in Paris?

a) *Chariots of Fire*

b) *Olympic Gold*

c) *Swifter, Higher, Stronger*

5 Who was the only British woman to win a track gold medal at the Olympics prior to Sally Gunnell in 1992?

a) Ann Packer

b) Lillian Board

c) Sonia Lannaman

6 Who won Great Britain's first gold medal at Beijing 2008?

a) Ben Ainslie

b) Sir Chris Hoy

c) Nicole Cooke

7 Who was Great Britain's top scorer in the hockey team that won gold in Seoul in 1988?

a) Stephen Batchelor

b) Sean Kerly

c) Ian Taylor

8 How many Olympic gold medals did Daley Thompson win in the decathlon?

a) One

b) Two

c) Three

9 In which event did Lynn Davies and Mary Rand win the men's and women's gold medals at the 1964 Olympics?

a) High jump

b) Long jump

c) Triple jump

10 What was double gold medallist Rebecca Adlington promised on her return to Mansfield from the 2008 Beijing Olympics?

a) A world cruise

b) Her own swimming pool

c) Designer shoes

A

1   a

2   c

3   b

4   a

5   a

6   c

7   b

8   b

9   b

10 c

TRACK

1   At which Olympics did Carl Lewis win three gold medals on the track?

a)   Los Angeles, 1984

b)   Seoul, 1988

c)   Barcelona, 1992

2   Usain Bolt won the sprint double at the 2008 Beijing Games, but which American athlete took bronze in both races?

a)   David Oliver

b)   Shawn Crawford

c)   Walter Dix

3   Which American athlete tumbled out of the women's 3,000m at the Los Angeles Olympics in 1984 after tripping over the heels of the British runner Zola Budd?

a)   Mary Decker

b)   Cindy Bremser

c)   Joan Hansen

4   Which Dutch athlete won gold at the London Games in 1948 in the 100m, 200m, 80m hurdles and 4 x 100m relay?

a)   Netty Witziers-Timmer

b)   Xenia Stad-de Jong

c)   Fanny Blankers-Koen

5   Which nation won 18 women's athletics medals at Seoul in 1988 – also the final time they competed in the Olympics?

a)   Soviet Union

b)   East Germany

c)   Yugoslavia

6 **At which Olympics did a unified team comprising former Soviet republics win 45 gold medals?**

a) Seoul, 1988

b) Barcelona, 1992

c) Atlanta, 1996

7 **At Athens 2004, which country prevented the USA from winning a clean sweep of the men's sprint medals by taking silver in the 100m?**

a) Jamaica

b) Portugal

c) Great Britain

8 **Which athlete became the first to win the 200m and the 400m in the same Olympics when he triumphed in Atlanta in 1996?**

a) Michael Johnson

b) Alvin Harrison

c) Derek Mills

9 **Which athlete was stripped of her five track medals from the 2000 Olympics in Sydney after admitting to taking performance-enhancing drugs?**

a) Florence Griffith Joyner

b) Merlene Ottey

c) Marion Jones

10 **What is the nationality of Kenenisa Bekele, who won the 5,000m and 10,000m at the 2008 Beijing Olympics?**

a) Ethiopian

b) Kenyan

c) Sudanese

A

1	a
2	c
3	a
4	c
5	b
6	b
7	b
8	a
9	c
10	a

FIELD

1 Sergey Bubka won the pole vault at six world championships, but at which Games did he win his only Olympics gold?

a) 1988

b) 1992

c) 1996

2 Which athlete set a world long jump record at the 1968 Olympics that stood until 1991?

a) Bob Beamon

b) Ralph Boston

c) Lynn Davies

3 Who won long jump gold in 1992 and 2000 to add to her three track and field medals from 1988?

a) Fiona May

b) Jackie Joyner-Kersee

c) Heike Drechsler

4 At which event did Jan Zelezny win Olympic gold in 1992, 1996 and 2000?

a) High jump

b) Javelin

c) Discus

5 What nationality is Irving Saladino, who won his country's only gold medal at the 2008 Beijing Games in the men's long jump?

a) Costa Rican

b) Panamanian

c) Portuguese

6 **In which event did Denise Lewis of Great Britain win gold at Sydney 2000, four years after taking bronze in Atlanta?**

a) Discus

b) Heptathlon

c) Javelin

7 **In which field event did Carl Lewis win four Olympic golds to add to his sprint medals?**

a) Long jump

b) High jump

c) Triple jump

8 **In which field event did Françoise Mbango Etone from Cameroon win her country's only gold medal in Beijing 2008?**

a) Triple jump

b) Pole vault

c) Hammer

A

9 **At which Olympics did Mary Peters win gold for Great Britain in the pentathlon?**

a) Munich, 1972

b) Montreal, 1976

c) Moscow, 1980

10 **Which Russian athlete took silver at Beijing 2008 in the women's long jump and triple jump?**

a) Tatyana Kotova

b) Tatyana Lebedeva

c) Tatyana Chernova

1	a
2	a
3	c
4	b
5	b
6	b
7	a
8	a
9	a
10	b

OUTSIDE THE STADIUM

1 The Czech Republic's Katerina Emmons won the first gold medal of the 2008 Beijing Games using which weapon?

a) Épée

b) Air rifle

c) Bow and arrow

2 Owing to Australian quarantine regulations, which city hosted the equestrian events during the 1956 Melbourne Olympics?

a) Stockholm

b) Hong Kong

c) Berlin

3 China won seven of the men's artistic gymnastics gold medals at Beijing 2008. Which country prevented them taking a clean sweep by winning the vault event?

a) Poland

b) Romania

c) Russia

4 At which Olympics did Tim Brabants win Britain's first canoeing gold medal?

a) Sydney, 2000

b) Athens, 2004

c) Beijing, 2008

5 Which nation won gold in both the men's singles and men's doubles tennis at Athens 2004?

a) Spain

b) Chile

c) Croatia

6 Which country has won the most hockey Olympic gold medals?

a) Netherlands

b) Pakistan

c) India

7 At which Olympics did Princess Anne compete as part of Great Britain's equestrian team?

a) Montreal, 1976

b) Moscow, 1980

c) Los Angeles, 1984

8 Which country has won the most archery gold medals since the sport returned to Olympic programme in 1972?

a) South Korea

b) France

c) Italy

9 In the men's cycling team pursuit in Athens 2004, Great Britain came second to which country?

a) Spain

b) Australia

c) Germany

10 Which country won five boxing gold medals at the Olympics in 2004, but none in 2008?

a) Russia

b) Cuba

c) USA

A

1	b
2	a
3	a
4	c
5	b
6	c
7	a
8	a
9	b
10	b

PARALYMPICS

1 At which Paralympics did wheelchair racer Chantal Petitclerc win the first of her 14 gold medals?

a) Barcelona, 1992

b) Atlanta, 1996

c) Sydney, 2000

2 Which country, along with the UK, competed in the first Paralympic Games in 1952?

a) Netherlands

b) Germany

c) Canada

3 Sarah Storey won cycling gold at Beijing 2008, but in which event did she first make her mark in the Paralympics?

a) Swimming

b) Athletics

c) Archery

4 Which Paralympian became a Dame of the British Empire in 2005?

a) Emma Brown

b) Deborah Criddle

c) Tanni Grey-Thompson

5 In which event did Natalie du Toit compete at the 2008 Beijing Olympics, prior to winning five swimming gold medals in the Beijing Paralympics?

a) Water polo

b) 10km open water race

c) 800m freestyle

6 Which Paralympian was chosen to carry the Team GB flag at the closing ceremony for Beijing 2008?

a) Darren Kenny

b) David Roberts

c) Aileen McGlynn

7 Which is the newest Paralympic event, introduced to the programme for Beijing 2008?

a) Basketball

b) Rowing

c) Tennis

8 In which year did the Paralympic Games first take place in the same city as the Olympic Games?

a) 1988

b) 1992

c) 1996

9 Which Paralympian is known as 'Blade Runner' because of his blade-shaped prosthetic legs?

a) Jerome Singleton

b) Marlon Shirley

c) Oscar Pistorius

10 Which country finished top of the medals table at the first Winter Paralympics in 1976?

a) Switzerland

b) West Germany

c) Norway

A

1	b
2	a
3	a
4	c
5	b
6	b
7	b
8	a
9	c
10	b

WINTER OLYMPICS

1 At which Winter Olympics did curling become established as a medal sport?

a) Oslo, 1952

b) Innsbruck, 1964

c) Nagano, 1998

2 In which year was the 'international winter sports week' – retrospectively recognised as the first Winter Olympics – held?

a) 1908

b) 1924

c) 1936

3 Which venue was the first outside Europe and the USA to host the Winter Olympics?

a) Valle Nevado

b) Nagano

c) Sapporo

4 In which sport did Great Britain win their only Olympic medal at Vancouver 2010?

a) Curling

b) Skeleton

c) Bobsleigh

5 Which country scored a surprise victory by winning ice hockey gold in 1998, the first year that professional players from the North American National Hockey League were allowed to compete?

a) Russia

b) Czech Republic

c) Finland

6 In which year did Jayne Torvill and Christopher Dean win gold for Great Britain in ice dancing?

a) 1976

b) 1980

c) 1984

7 Which country took the gold medal at the first six Winter Olympic Games in the men's normal hill individual ski jump?

a) Norway

b) Sweden

c) Austria

8 Which country won its only two-man bobsleigh medal (a bronze) at the 1968 Winter Olympics in Grenoble?

a) Romania

b) Jamaica

c) Argentina

9 How many Winter Olympic gold medals were won by the legendary Austrian downhill skier Franz Klammer?

a) One

b) Three

c) Five

10 What was the nickname of Eddie Edwards, Great Britain's first Winter Olympics ski jumper?

a) The Elephant

b) The Eagle

c) The Albatross

A

1	c
2	b
3	c
4	b
5	b
6	c
7	a
8	a
9	a
10	b

BACK IN TIME

At which Olympic Games did the following sports make their last appearance?

1 Rugby union
a) 1900
b) 1924
c) 1948

2 Dog sled racing
a) 1924
b) 1932
c) 1948

3 Croquet
a) 1900
b) 1936
c) 1948

4 Polo
a) 1936
b) 1948
c) 1964

5 Gliding
a) 1936
b) 1958
c) 1964

6 Roller hockey
a) 1948
b) 1964
c) 1992

7 Water skiing
a) 1972
b) 1984
c) 1992

8 Golf
a) 1904
b) 1924
c) 1948

9 Korfball
a) 1904
b) 1928
c) 1936

10 Tug of war
a) 1900
b) 1904
c) 1920

A

1 b
2 b
3 a
4 a
5 a
6 c
7 a
8 a
9 b
10 c

MOTORSPORT

FORMULA ONE

1 In which Grand Prix did Jenson Button secure the 2009 drivers' title?

a) Brazil

b) Abu Dhabi

c) Australia

2 Which driver in 1982 equalled Mike Hawthorn's record of winning the world championship despite having won only one Grand Prix all season?

a) Alain Prost

b) Nelson Piquet

c) Keke Rosberg

3 In which year did Michael Schumacher win his first world title?

a) 1994

b) 1995

c) 1996

4 Which country holds the record for most wins in the World Drivers' Championship?

a) Germany

b) Great Britain

c) Brazil

5 What colour flag is displayed to warn a driver that he is about to be lapped and should let the faster car overtake?

a) Yellow

b) Blue

c) White

MOTORSPORT

6 Which British driver began his career with Hesketh Racing and went on to become world champion with the McLaren team in 1976?

a) James Hunt

b) John Watson

c) Nigel Mansell

7 Which driver equalled Jim Clark's record of five British Grand Prix wins when he won the race in 1993?

a) Ayrton Senna

b) Riccardo Patrese

c) Alain Prost

8 What was unique about Jochen Rindt's world championship victory in 1970?

a) He failed to score a point from the first six races

b) He scored a record number of Grand Prix wins

c) It was awarded posthumously

9 What nationality is Robert Kubica, who became his country's first Formula One representative in 2006 and won his first Grand Prix two years later?

a) Croatian

b) Czech

c) Polish

10 Prior to Lewis Hamilton and Jenson Button, who were the last drivers to win back-to-back world titles for Great Britain?

a) Graham Hill and Jackie Stewart

b) Graham Hill and Jim Clark

c) Damon Hill and Nigel Mansell

A

1	a
2	c
3	a
4	b
5	b
6	a
7	c
8	c
9	c
10	a

SUPERBIKES AND MOTO GP

1 Which rider won a record four World Superbike Championship titles, all during the 1990s?

a) Doug Polen

b) Troy Corser

c) Carl Fogarty

2 In which class of motorcycle racing did Eric Oliver win four world championships in the 1940s and 1950s?

a) Sidecar

b) 50cc

c) 125cc

3 Which legend of motorcycle racing also embarked on a career in Formula One, and was awarded the George Medal for rescuing Clay Regazzoni from a burning car at the 1973 South African Grand Prix?

a) Barry Sheene

b) Phil Read

c) Mike Hailwood

4 Who won the 2009 World Superbike Championship in his first season?

a) Max Biaggi

b) Noriyuki Haga

c) Ben Spies

5 Which flamboyant rider came back from a career-threatening crash in 1975 to win the world championships at 500cc in the following two seasons?

a) Kenny Roberts

b) Barry Sheene

c) Phil Read

6 **Which rider in 1991 set a record of 17 World Superbike wins in the same season?**

a) Colin Edwards

b) Raymond Roche

c) Doug Polen

7 **Who followed his father into motorcycle racing and won seven world titles between 2001 and 2009?**

a) Valentino Rossi

b) Jorge Lorenzo

c) Marco Simoncelli

8 **Which rider won a hat-trick of British Superbike Championship titles from 1996 to 1998?**

a) Terry Rymer

b) Niall Mackenzie

c) John Reynolds

9 **Which rider won seven successive motorcycle world championships at 350cc and 500cc in the 1960s and 1970s?**

a) Giacomo Agostini

b) Kenny Roberts

c) Michael Doohan

10 **Which circuit on the British Superbikes schedule is a former airfield that was used during the D-Day landings?**

a) Mallory Park

b) Cadwell Park

c) Thruxton

A

1	c
2	a
3	c
4	c
5	b
6	c
7	a
8	b
9	a
10	c

RALLYING

---

1 Who was the first British driver to win the World Rally Championship?

a) Roger Clark

b) Colin McRae

c) Richard Burns

---

2 Which manufacturer has won the most World Rally Championship titles?

a) Lancia

b) Alfa Romeo

c) Subaru

---

3 Drivers from which country have won the most World Rally Championship titles?

a) France

b) Finland

c) Italy

---

4 From 2000, which city became the regular home of the British leg of the World Rally Championship?

a) Edinburgh

b) Cardiff

c) York

---

5 Which eastern European country was added to the World Rally Championship schedule for the first time in 2010?

a) Czech Republic

b) Poland

c) Bulgaria

MOTORSPORT

6 Which driver followed up his second place in the 2002 Monte Carlo Rally by winning the event five times between 2003 and 2008?

a) Sébastien Ogier

b) Tommi Makinen

c) Sébastien Loeb

---

7 Which driver set a record for the closest win when he edged out Sébastien Loeb by 0.3 seconds to win Rally New Zealand in 2007?

a) Marcus Gronholm

b) Carlos Sainz

c) Petter Solberg

---

8 Who set the record as the oldest winner of a World Rally Championship event when he won the Safari Rally in 1990 at the age of 46 years and 155 days?

a) Hannu Mikkola

b) Bjorn Waldegard

c) Ingvar Carlsson

---

9 In which country is Dakar, traditional destination of the famous international rally first held in 1979?

a) Senegal

b) Nigeria

c) Morocco

---

10 Which continent hosted the Dakar Rally in 2009 after cancellation in 2008 because of terrorism fears?

a) North America

b) Asia

c) South America

A

1	b
2	a
3	b
4	b
5	c
6	c
7	a
8	b
9	a
10	c

SPEEDWAY

---

1 Which country hosted the inaugural World Cup that replaced the World Team Cup in 2001?

a) Poland

b) Great Britain

c) Denmark

---

2 Which country in 1989 ended Denmark's run of six consecutive wins in the World Team Cup?

a) USA

b) Sweden

c) England

---

3 Which country won the World Cup three times in five years from 2005 to 2009?

a) Australia

b) Poland

c) Czech Republic

---

4 Which was the first city outside London to host the final of the individual World Speedway Championship?

a) Bradford

b) Malmo

c) Los Angeles

---

5 Which rider in 2005 equalled Ivan Mauger's record of six individual World Speedway Championship wins?

a) Tony Rickardsson

b) Nicki Pedersen

c) Jason Crump

6 **Which team was the first to win the Elite League when it was established as Great Britain's senior speedway competition in 1997?**

a) Ipswich Witches

b) Eastbourne Eagles

c) Bradford Dukes

7 **Which town is home to the Pirates, who in 2008 won the Elite League for a record third time?**

a) Peterborough

b) Poole

c) Pontefract

8 **Who was the first rider from New Zealand to win the individual World Championship?**

a) Ronnie Moore

b) Ivan Mauger

c) Barry Briggs

9 **After which rider is the World Cup trophy named?**

a) Hans Nielsen

b) Ove Fundin

c) Ole Olsen

10 **What nationality is Matej Zagar, who in 2008 became the first rider to win the European Speedway Championship twice?**

a) Slovenian

b) Polish

c) Ukrainian

A

1	a
2	c
3	b
4	b
5	a
6	c
7	b
8	a
9	b
10	a

CIRCUIT FEATURES

At which race circuits would you find the following features?

1 Hailwood Rise

a) Donington Park

b) Isle of Man TT

c) Cadwell Park

2 The Esses

a) Mallory Park

b) Donington Park

c) Silverstone

3 Stowe

a) Silverstone

b) Brands Hatch

c) Thruxton

4 Druids Bend

a) Brands Hatch

b) Brooklands

c) Croft

5 Mur du Quebec

a) Istanbul Park

b) Gilles Villeneuve, Montreal

c) Magny-Cours

6 Haug Hook

a) Österreichring

b) Spa-Francorchamps

c) Nürburgring

7 Grand Hotel Hairpin

a) Monaco

b) Interlagos

c) Sepang

8 Kemmel Straight

a) Spa-Francorchamps

b) Detroit

c) Suzuka

9 Parabolica Ayrton Senna

a) Hungaroring

b) Estoril

c) Shanghai

10 Variante Ascari

a) Monza

b) Imola

c) Kyalami

A

1	b
2	b
3	a
4	a
5	b
6	c
7	a
8	a
9	b
10	a

RUGBY LEAGUE

SUPER LEAGUE

1 Which was the first French team to play in Super League?

a) Paris St-Germain

b) Catalans Dragons

c) Toulouse

2 Who holds the record for the most goals (including drop goals) scored in a single Super League season?

a) Andy Farrell

b) Sean Long

c) Henry Paul

3 What name did Halifax adopt in readiness for the creation of the Super League?

a) Halifax Hunters

b) Halifax Redcoats

c) Halifax Blue Sox

4 Who scored a record 2,228 points in his Super League career before leaving the game to play rugby union in 2004?

a) Jason Robinson

b) Andy Farrell

c) Henry Paul

5 Against which team did Iestyn Harris of the Leeds Rhinos score a Super League record of 42 points in one match in July 1999?

a) Salford City Reds

b) Huddersfield Giants

c) Widnes Vikings

6 **In which season did the size of Super League increase from 12 teams to 14?**

a) 2007

b) 2008

c) 2009

7 **Which player set a record in 2004 for the most tries in a Super League regular season?**

a) Lesley Vainikolo

b) Danny McGuire

c) Mark Calderwood

8 **Which stadium in 2007 hosted the first Super League 'Magic Weekend'?**

a) Murrayfield

b) Old Trafford

c) Millennium Stadium

9 **Which town is home to the Catalans Dragons?**

a) Montpellier

b) Béziers

c) Perpignan

10 **Which team finished top of Super League four years running from 2005 to 2008 but only managed to win one of the play-off Grand Finals?**

a) Wigan Warriors

b) St Helens

c) Leeds Rhinos

A

1 a

2 c

3 c

4 b

5 b

6 c

7 a

8 c

9 c

10 b

CHALLENGE CUP

1   Who were the first winners of the Challenge Cup?

a)   Leeds

b)   Rochdale

c)   Batley

2   In which year was the final first played at Wembley?

a)   1929

b)   1938

c)   1948

3   Which team was the first to win a replayed Challenge Cup final?

a)   Leeds

b)   Hull FC

c)   Bradford

4   Which team recorded a record eight consecutive Challenge Cup final wins from 1988 to 1995?

a)   Hull Kingston Rovers

b)   St Helens

c)   Wigan

5   Who became the first French team to reach the final in 2007?

a)   Toulouse Olympique

b)   Catalans Dragons

c)   Béziers XIII

6 Which stadium hosted the final in 2000 when Wembley closed for redevelopment?

a) Twickenham

b) Murrayfield

c) Millennium Stadium

7 Which player has made the most Challenge Cup final appearances?

a) Roger Millward

b) Martin Offiah

c) Shaun Edwards

8 Who was the first player to be named man of the match in the final on three separate occasions?

a) Sean Long

b) Shaun Edwards

c) Ellery Hanley

9 Which team won the first Challenge Cup Plate in 1997, introduced for teams knocked out in the early rounds?

a) Hull Kingston Rovers

b) Dewsbury

c) Workington

10 Which rugby league team hosts a celebratory dinner for the man of the match in the final?

a) Salford

b) Huddersfield

c) Wakefield

A

1	c
2	a
3	a
4	c
5	b
6	b
7	c
8	a
9	a
10	a

THE INTERNATIONAL GAME

---

1   Which team won the World Club Challenge three times between 2002 and 2006?

a)   Brisbane Broncos

b)   Melbourne Storm

c)   Bradford Bulls

---

2   Which country won the first World Cup in 1954?

a)   Great Britain

b)   Australia

c)   New Zealand

---

3   In which year did the Cook Islands, Russia and Lebanon make their only appearances in the final stages of the World Cup?

a)   1988

b)   1995

c)   2000

---

4   Who captained Great Britain to win the World Cup in 1972?

a)   Eric Ashton

b)   Roger Millward

c)   Clive Sullivan

---

5   Which country recorded the biggest winning margin in the World Cup, beating Russia 110–4 in 2000?

a)   France

b)   Australia

c)   New Zealand

6 **Which nation won the Mediterranean Cup on the four occasions that it was contested?**

a) Lebanon

b) Morocco

c) Italy

7 **Which Great Britain player received the fastest dismissal in the history of rugby league Tests when he was sent off after just 12 seconds against Australia in 2003?**

a) Paul Sculthorpe

b) Adrian Morley

c) Sean Long

8 **Which country won the World Cup for the first time in 2008?**

a) France

b) England

c) New Zealand

9 **Which nation was invited to join England, Australia and New Zealand in the 2009 Four Nations tournament?**

a) Scotland

b) France

c) Ireland

10 **Which country hosted and won the 2009 Pacific Cup?**

a) Samoa

b) Tonga

c) Papua New Guinea

A

1 c

2 a

3 c

4 c

5 b

6 a

7 b

8 c

9 b

10 c

HISTORY OF THE GAME

In which years did the following rugby league events occur?

1 Abolition of line-outs

a) 1897

b) 1960

c) 1994

2 Introduction of Super League

a) 1995

b) 1996

c) 1997

3 Formation of the Northern Rugby Football Union, prior to the Rugby Football League

a) 1895

b) 1910

c) 1925

4 First World Cup

a) 1954

b) 1960

c) 1968

5 Introduction of two divisions

a) 1898

b) 1902

c) 1948

6 Ellery Hanley transferred from Wigan to Leeds

a) 1987

b) 1989

c) 1991

7 Introduction of the Australian rugby league State of Origin series

a) 1975

b) 1978

c) 1980

8 Introduction of the six tackle rule

a) 1972

b) 1982

c) 1992

9 Move to a summer season

a) 1991

b) 1996

c) 1999

10 Sin bin introduced

a) 1983

b) 1993

c) 2003

A

1 a

2 b

3 a

4 a

5 b

6 c

7 c

8 a

9 b

10 a

OTHER SPORTS

AMERICAN SPORT

1 Which ice hockey legend famously wore the number 99 shirt and was known as 'the Great One'?

a) Gordie Howe

b) Wayne Gretzky

c) Mario Lemieux

2 With which team did Babe Ruth begin his major league baseball career?

a) Boston Red Sox

b) Chicago White Sox

c) California Angels

3 Which team beat the Kansas City Chiefs in the first Super Bowl?

a) Green Bay Packers

b) Buffalo Bills

c) Dallas Cowboys

4 With which team did record-breaking quarterback Dan Marino spend his NFL career?

a) Oakland Raiders

b) Pittsburgh Steelers

c) Miami Dolphins

5 Which basketball player came out of retirement to join the Washington Wizards, having previously captained the Chicago Bulls?

a) Michael Jordan

b) Shaquille O'Neal

c) Larry Bird

6 How many teams competed in the inaugural season of the National Hockey League in 1917?

a) Four

b) Eight

c) Ten

7 Which city was the home of the Lakers basketball team before Los Angeles?

a) New Orleans

b) Minneapolis

c) Portland

8 Which player led the San Francisco 49ers to four Super Bowl titles, winning the MVP three times?

a) Joe Montana

b) John Elway

c) Brett Favre

A

9 Which team won the first baseball World Series in 1903?

a) Atlanta Braves

b) Boston Red Sox

c) St Louis Cardinals

10 Players from which baseball team were banned for life after a gambling scandal in 1919?

a) Chicago White Sox

b) New York Mets

c) Texas Rangers

1	b
2	a
3	a
4	c
5	a
6	a
7	b
8	a
9	b
10	a

ATHLETICS

1   Who won the women's marathon at the 2005 World Athletics Championships?

a)   Catherine Ndereba

b)   Reiko Tosa

c)   Paula Radcliffe

2   Who was the first man to break the 10-second barrier in the 100m?

a)   Jim Hines

b)   Robert Hayes

c)   Allan Wells

3   Which British runner won the men's 1,500m at the first World Athletics Championships in 1983?

a)   Steve Ovett

b)   Sebastian Coe

c)   Steve Cram

4   What was the original name of the Commonwealth Games?

a)   British Empire Games

b)   British Commonwealth Games

c)   Queen's Games

5   Which British runner set a European Athletics Championship record for the 400m when the event was held in Budapest in 1998?

a)   Iwan Thomas

b)   Roger Black

c)   John Regis

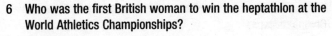

6 Who was the first British woman to win the heptathlon at the World Athletics Championships?

a) Jessica Ennis

b) Mary Peters

c) Denise Lewis

7 Which nation made a clean sweep of the gold medals in the men's and women's 100m and 200m at the 2006 Commonwealth Games?

a) South Africa

b) Australia

c) Jamaica

8 Which country is second behind the USA in the all-time medals table for the Pan American Games?

a) Cuba

b) Argentina

c) Canada

9 What is the standard distance for a sprint race at an indoor athletics meeting?

a) 60m

b) 80m

c) 100m

10 Which British city will host the 2014 Commonwealth Games?

a) Birmingham

b) Glasgow

c) Cardiff

A

1 c

2 a

3 c

4 a

5 a

6 a

7 c

8 a

9 a

10 b

BADMINTON

1 In which English county is Badminton Hall, from which the game takes its name?

a) Surrey

b) Hertfordshire

c) Gloucestershire

2 What is the more familiar title of the International Badminton Championship Challenge Cup?

a) The Thomas Cup

b) The Uber Cup

c) The Sudirman Cup

3 Who partnered Nathan Robertson to a silver medal for Great Britain in the badminton mixed doubles at the 2004 Olympics in Athens?

a) Gail Emms

b) Donna Kellogg

c) Kelly Morgan

4 Which Indian city hosted the 2009 World Badminton Championships, from which the England team withdrew because of security concerns?

a) Bangalore

b) Mumbai

c) Hyderabad

5 Which country has dominated the World Championships since they began in 1977, including winning all five events in 1987?

a) Denmark

b) China

c) USA

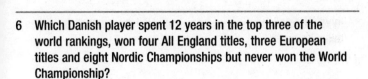

6 **Which Danish player spent 12 years in the top three of the world rankings, won four All England titles, three European titles and eight Nordic Championships but never won the World Championship?**

a) Thomas Lund

b) Steen Fladberg

c) Morten Frost

7 **In which year was badminton first contested as an official Olympic sport?**

a) 1992

b) 1996

c) 2000

8 **Which country won gold in the men's and women's singles when the sport made its debut in the Olympics?**

a) India

b) Indonesia

c) South Korea

9 **Which event was introduced by the Badminton World Federation in 2007 to raise the profile of the sport internationally?**

a) World Challenge

b) Super League

c) Super Series

10 **How high is a badminton net at its centre?**

a) 1.37m (4ft 6in)

b) 1.42m (4ft 8in)

c) 1.52m (5ft)

A

1 c

2 a

3 a

4 c

5 b

6 c

7 a

8 b

9 c

10 c

BASKETBALL

1 **Which town in Massachusetts is home to the USA's Basketball Hall of Fame?**

a) Springfield

b) Worcester

c) Boston

2 **Which African country is the birthplace of top British player Luol Deng?**

a) Nigeria

b) Algeria

c) Sudan

3 **Which nation inflicted the first Olympic men's basketball defeat on the USA in the controversial final of the 1972 Munich Games?**

a) Soviet Union

b) Argentina

c) Cuba

4 **Which legendary player led the Chicago Bulls to six National Basketball Association titles in eight years during the 1990s?**

a) Michael Jordan

b) Magic Johnson

c) Shaquille O'Neal

5 **For which British club did the NBA star Dennis Rodman play three games after his appearance on Celebrity Big Brother in 2006?**

a) Guildford Heat

b) Sheffield Sharks

c) Brighton Bears

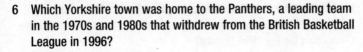

6 Which Yorkshire town was home to the Panthers, a leading team in the 1970s and 1980s that withdrew from the British Basketball League in 1996?

a) Doncaster

b) Pontefract

c) Huddersfield

7 Which US city was the original home of the team now known as Utah Jazz?

a) Atlanta

b) New Orleans

c) Memphis

8 According to regulations, how high should the basketball hoop be from the ground?

a) 2.44m (8ft)

b) 2.74m (9ft)

c) 3.05m (10ft)

9 Which nation won the first world championship in 1950?

a) USA

b) Argentina

c) East Germany

10 Which NBA record is held by the former player 'Muggsy' Bogues?

a) Tallest player

b) Shortest player

c) Most appearances

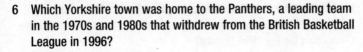

A

1	a
2	c
3	a
4	a
5	c
6	a
7	b
8	c
9	b
10	b

CURLING

---

1 In 2006 which curling team won gold 82 years late when the International Olympic Committee decided to award retrospective medals for the 1924 Games?

a) Canada

b) Great Britain

c) Norway

---

2 Which city is home to the Royal Caledonian Curling Club, the governing body for the sport in Scotland?

a) Perth

b) Edinburgh

c) Aberdeen

---

3 What is the name of the curling contest between the north and the south of Scotland, held on a frozen loch when the weather is cold enough?

a) The Grand Match

b) The Curling Challenge

c) Scotland's Pride

---

4 In which country do players compete in the Brier to win the right to represent their nation in the World Curling Championships?

a) Canada

b) USA

c) Sweden

---

5 What was the original name of the World Curling Championships when the event was launched in 1959?

a) The Scotch Cup

b) The World Series

c) The Canadian Challenge

6 How many teams contested the first World Mixed Doubles Curling Championships in 2008?

a) 12

b) 16

c) 24

7 Which city hosted the European Curling Championships in 2009?

a) Aberdeen

b) Glasgow

c) Dundee

8 Which country has won the most medals at the World Curling Championships?

a) USA

b) Scotland

c) Canada

9 Which monarch approved the title of the Royal Caledonian Curling Club?

a) Edward VII

b) Queen Victoria

c) George V

10 What nationality is Eva Lund, who won two gold medals, two silver medals and a bronze medal at the World Curling Championships between 2001 and 2009?

a) Finnish

b) Swedish

c) Danish

A

1	b
2	b
3	a
4	a
5	a
6	c
7	a
8	c
9	b
10	b

CYCLING

1 Which award was added to the Tour de France in 1933?

a) King of the Mountains

b) Points classification

c) Best young rider

2 Which British cyclist won gold at the 1992 Olympics on a bike built by the Lotus car company?

a) Chris Hoy

b) Pat Kinch

c) Chris Boardman

3 Who was the first cyclist to use aerobars on his bike in the Tour de France?

a) Miguel Indurain

b) Laurent Fignon

c) Greg LeMond

4 Which British cyclist partnered Victoria Pendleton to the gold medal in the women's team sprint at the 2008 World Championships?

a) Shanaze Reade

b) Elizabeth Armitstead

c) Joanna Rowsell

5 In which city did the first Tour de France start and finish?

a) Nice

b) Marseille

c) Paris

6 **Which country finished top of the medals table at the World Track Cycling Championships in 2007 and 2008?**

a) Spain

b) Netherlands

c) Great Britain

7 **In the Tour de France, what colour jersey is awarded for sprint points?**

a) Yellow

b) Green

c) Blue

8 **In 1927 which motor racing circuit became the venue for the first Road World Championships?**

a) Monza

b) Spa

c) Nürburgring

9 **Graeme Obree used parts from which household appliance to build the bike on which he broke the world hour record?**

a) Record player

b) TV

c) Washing machine

10 **Which cyclist holds the record for most wins in the Tour de France, with seven?**

a) Eddy Merckx

b) Lance Armstrong

c) Fausto Coppi

A

1 a

2 c

3 c

4 a

5 c

6 c

7 b

8 c

9 c

10 b

DARTS

1 Which year saw the introduction of two world championship tournaments – one under the British Darts Organisation and the other under the Professional Darts Corporation?

a) 1994

b) 1996

c) 1998

2 Who won the last world title before the split?

a) John Lowe

b) Phil Taylor

c) Bob Anderson

3 Who was the first player from outside the UK to win a world title?

a) John Part

b) Raymond van Barneveld

c) Tony David

4 Which Yorkshire cricket legend hosted the TV show *Indoor League*, which featured one of the earliest televised darts tournaments?

a) Geoff Boycott

b) Fred Trueman

c) Brian Close

5 Which newspaper sponsored a famous darts tournament that ran from 1927 until the 1990s and gave pub players the chance to compete against the game's elite?

a) *News of the World*

b) *The Guardian*

c) *The Sun*

6 **What nationality is Leo Laurens, who was the World Darts Federation number one player in 1993?**

a) Belgian

b) Dutch

c) Swedish

7 **Who won the first seven British Darts Organisation's women's world titles?**

a) Francis Hoenselaar

b) Trina Gulliver

c) Anne Kirk

8 **Which player recorded 48 scores of 180 on his way to the 2000 British Darts Organisation title?**

a) Steve Beaton

b) Ted Hankey

c) Martin Adams

9 **Who won the inaugural World Professional Darts Championship in 1978?**

a) Leighton Rees

b) John Lowe

c) Eric Bristow

10 **Which world champion is known as 'the Power'?**

a) Jocky Wilson

b) Keith Deller

c) Phil Taylor

A

1	a
2	a
3	a
4	b
5	a
6	a
7	b
8	b
9	a
10	c

EQUESTRIANISM

1 Why was the team showjumping event at the 1932 Olympics in Los Angeles declared void?

a) Quarantine problems

b) No nation had three riders complete the course

c) Bad weather

2 Which British eventer has won two gold medals in the World Championships, four at the European Championships and a record six Badminton Horse Trials on six different horses?

a) Lucinda Green

b) Richard Meade

c) Mark Phillips

3 Which Irish rider won the Hickstead Derby four years in a row during the 1970s?

a) Paul Darragh

b) Eddie Macken

c) Seamus Hayes

4 Which venue hosts the Horse of the Year Show?

a) Wembley Arena

b) Olympia

c) The NEC

5 Which country won the most medals for equestrian events at the 2008 Beijing Olympics?

a) Germany

b) Great Britain

c) New Zealand

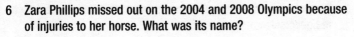

6 Zara Phillips missed out on the 2004 and 2008 Olympics because of injuries to her horse. What was its name?

a) Primmore's Pride

b) Tankers Town

c) Toytown

7 What is the name of the equestrian equivalent of the high jump, in which the height of the fences is increased for every round?

a) Steeplechase

b) Puissance

c) Vaulting

8 Who in 2004 won Britain's first Olympic gold medal in equestrian events since Richard Meade in 1972?

a) Leslie Law

b) Mary King

c) Pippa Funnell

9 Which rider won the BBC Sports Personality of the Year Award in 1971?

a) Virginia Leng

b) Harvey Smith

c) Princess Anne

10 Which equestrian discipline was originally referred to as 'militaire'?

a) Dressage

b) Eventing

c) Showjumping

A

1   b

2   a

3   b

4   c

5   a

6   c

7   b

8   a

9   c

10 b

FENCING

1 In competitive fencing, which weapon has the highest maximum weight?

a) Foil

b) Épée

c) Sabre

2 Which country has won the most Olympic gold medals in fencing since the sport was introduced to the 1896 Games?

a) Argentina

b) France

c) Italy

3 At which Olympic Games did Gillian Sheen win Great Britain's only gold medal for fencing?

a) 1956

b) 1964

c) 1980

4 Which Italian fencer was banned from the 2008 Beijing Olympics for failing a drugs test, but after being cleared returned in 2009 to win gold medals at the World and European Championships?

a) Salvatore Sanzo

b) Andrea Baldini

c) Andrea Cassarà

5 Which solo singer won a fencing scholarship to pay his way through college and reportedly uses fencing to warm up for his shows?

a) Bruce Springsteen

b) Neil Diamond

c) Alice Cooper

6 Which is the only African country to have won medals at the World Fencing Championships?

a) Tunisia

b) South Africa

c) Egypt

7 The singer of which rock band is an accomplished fencer and founded a business selling fencing equipment?

a) Bruce Dickinson (Iron Maiden)

b) Robert Plant (Led Zeppelin)

c) Eric Bloom (Blue Öyster Cult)

8 In the event of a tie, what is the name of a fence-off to decide a match?

a) Tie-break

b) Cut

c) Barrage

9 Which nation won all three Olympic medals in the women's individual sabre event in Beijing 2008 but only won bronze in the team competition?

a) France

b) China

c) USA

10 What is the name of the move in which a fencer drops one hand to the floor and ducks under the oncoming blade?

a) Passata-sotto

b) Flèche

c) Parry

A

1	b
2	c
3	a
4	b
5	b
6	c
7	a
8	c
9	c
10	a

FIVES

---

1 Who provided Eton's opposition for their first school challenge in 1885?

a) Rugby

b) Westminster

c) Harrow

---

2 In which year did the first Eton Fives Varsity match take place?

a) 1928

b) 1933

c) 1938

---

3 Which form of Eton Fives held its first championship in 1985?

a) Men's doubles

b) Ladies' singles

c) Mixed doubles

---

4 How many walls are used for a Rugby Fives court?

a) One

b) Three

c) Five

---

5 In which version of the game do players compete for the Jesters' Cup?

a) Rugby Fives

b) Eton Fives

c) Winchester Fives

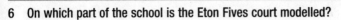

6   On which part of the school is the Eton Fives court modelled?

a)   The chapel

b)   The Eton Wall Game playing area

c)   The central tower

7   What is thought to be the origin of the word 'Fives'?

a)   The number of players in a team when the game originated

b)   The number of games played to complete a set

c)   The number of digits on a hand

8   At which school was a Fives association founded in 1927?

a)   Marlborough

b)   Rugby

c)   Winchester

9   Field Marshal Bernard Montgomery is said to have proposed to his wife on the Fives court of which school?

a)   Cheltenham

b)   Shrewsbury

c)   Charterhouse

10 At which school was the author Roald Dahl captain of Fives?

a)   Clifton

b)   Repton

c)   Eton

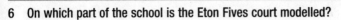

OTHER SPORTS

A

1   c

2   a

3   c

4   b

5   a

6   a

7   c

8   b

9   c

10   b

GAELIC GAMES

1   **Which stadium in Dublin is the venue for the all-Ireland hurling and Gaelic football finals?**

a)   Tolka Park

b)   Dalymount Park

c)   Croke Park

2   **Why didn't the Kerry team contest the 1910 all-Ireland Gaelic football final against Louth?**

a)   Player illness

b)   The match was on a Sunday

c)   Dispute with a rail company

3   **Which trophy is awarded to the all-Ireland hurling champions?**

a)   Liam McCarthy Cup

b)   Sam Maguire Cup

c)   Christy Ring Cup

4   **With which county did the former Irish prime minister Jack Lynch win all-Ireland hurling and Gaelic football finals?**

a)   Waterford

b)   Kilkenny

c)   Cork

5   **Which county has the most wins in the all-Ireland Gaelic football final, including five between 2000 and 2009?**

a)   Donegal

b)   Kerry

c)   Tyrone

6   What is the name of the ball in hurling?

a)   Hurley

b)   Sliotar

c)   Puc

7   Against which country has Ireland played a series of Gaelic football matches under a composite set of rules?

a)   Australia

b)   USA

c)   Sweden

8   Which city in 1947 hosted the only all-Ireland Gaelic football final to be played outside the country?

a)   New York

b)   Boston

c)   Sydney

9   What is the name of the women's version of hurling?

a)   Caman

b)   Shinty

c)   Camogie

10 How many points is a goal worth in both hurling and Gaelic football?

a)   One

b)   Three

c)   Five

A

1	c
2	c
3	a
4	c
5	b
6	b
7	a
8	a
9	c
10	b

GREYHOUND RACING

1 **Which venue originally hosted the English Greyhound Derby?**

a) Wimbledon

b) Walthamstow

c) White City

2 **Which double Derby winner starred alongside Bud Flanagan and Chesney Allen in the 1934 comedy film *Wild Boy*?**

a) Wild Woolley

b) Highland Rum

c) Mick the Miller

3 **Which dog became only the third runner to win the Derby twice with victories in 2000 and 2001?**

a) Westmead Hawk

b) Patricia's Hope

c) Rapid Ranger

4 **Which greyhound set a record of 20 successive wins in 1974?**

a) Sarah's Bunny

b) Westpark Mustard

c) Indian Joe

5 **Which city hosted the first greyhound race in Great Britain in 1926?**

a) Manchester

b) London

c) Newcastle

6 Which country is credited with introducing greyhound racing to Great Britain?

a) Ireland

b) Germany

c) USA

7 Which trainer won the Derby four times between 1997 and 2003?

a) Charlie Lister

b) Seamus Cahill

c) Nick Savva

8 Which punk rocker raced a greyhound called Hersham Boy?

a) Gaye Advert

b) John Lydon

c) Jimmy Pursey

9 Which greyhound lost his first four races but went on to set a world record of 32 consecutive wins between 1985 and 1986?

a) Tico

b) Ballyregan Bob

c) Lone Wolf

10 Which track hosts the Greyhound Grand National?

a) Wimbledon

b) Perry Barr

c) Crayford

A

1 c

2 c

3 c

4 b

5 a

6 c

7 a

8 c

9 b

10 a

GYMNASTICS

1 Which gymnastics event became a medal sport at the Olympics in 2000?

a) Club swinging

b) Trampolining

c) Rhythmic gymnastics

2 In which event at the 2008 Beijing Olympics did Louis Smith win the first gymnastics medal for Great Britain since 1928?

a) Floor

b) Horizontal bar

c) Pommel horse

3 Which gymnast became known as 'the Sparrow from Minsk'?

a) Nellie Kim

b) Ludmilla Tourischeva

c) Olga Korbut

4 When the Soviet bloc boycotted the 1984 Olympics, who became the first gymnast from outside eastern Europe to win the women's individual all-around competition?

a) Mary Lou Retton

b) Kathy Johnson

c) Julianne McNamara

5 In 2008 Michael Phelps became the most decorated male Olympian with a total of 16 medals. Which gymnast held the record before him?

a) Boris Shakhlin

b) Vitaly Scherbo

c) Nikolai Andrianov

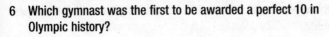

6 Which gymnast was the first to be awarded a perfect 10 in Olympic history?

a) Nellie Kim

b) Olga Korbut

c) Nadia Comaneci

7 Under international rules, what is the maximum permitted time for a routine on the balance beam?

a) 90sec

b) 120sec

c) 150sec

8 For which country did Kyle Shewfelt win a first gymnastics gold medal at the 2004 Athens Olympics?

a) Australia

b) Canada

c) New Zealand

9 Who in 2009 became the first Briton to win a medal in the men's all-around event at the World Artistic Gymnastics Championships?

a) Louis Smith

b) Daniel Keatings

c) Kristian Thomas

10 Which venue will host gymnastics events at the London Olympics in 2012?

a) Earls Court

b) The O2 Arena

c) Wembley Arena

A

1 b

2 c

3 c

4 a

5 c

6 c

7 a

8 b

9 b

10 b

HOCKEY AND LACROSSE

1 In which year did Great Britain Hockey introduce a Super League to help identify potential Olympic team members?

a) 2005

b) 2006

c) 2007

2 Which member of Great Britain's Olympic champion hockey team of 1988 became England's most capped player?

a) Richard Leman

b) Sean Kerly

c) Stephen Batchelor

3 In which area of London was the first hockey club formed in 1849?

a) Blackheath

b) Teddington

c) Hurlingham

4 Who captained the Australian women's hockey team to three Olympic gold medals, two World Cups and five Champions Trophies?

a) Sally Carbon

b) Jackie Pereira

c) Rechelle Hawkes

5 What colour card is shown by a hockey umpire to indicate that a player has been warned for their behaviour?

a) Yellow

b) Red

c) Green

6 **In which year did Major League Lacrosse become established in the USA?**

a) 1988

b) 1995

c) 2001

---

7 **What is the height of the crossbar for a hockey goal?**

a) 1.52m (5ft)

b) 1.83m (6ft)

c) 2.14m (7ft)

---

8 **How many players constitute a team for indoor lacrosse?**

a) Six

b) Seven

c) Eight

---

9 **Which country hosted the inaugural men's Hockey World Cup in 1971?**

a) India

b) Spain

c) Pakistan

---

10 **Which is the only team other than the USA to have won the World Lacrosse Championships?**

a) Canada

b) Iceland

c) Peru

A

1	c
2	a
3	a
4	c
5	c
6	c
7	c
8	a
9	b
10	a

ICE SKATING

1 What was Christopher Dean's job before he found fame in an ice dance partnership with Jayne Torvill?

a) Policeman

b) Bus driver

c) Vet

2 At which Winter Games was short track speed skating upgraded to a full Olympic sport having previously been a demonstration event?

a) Sarajevo, 1984

b) Calgary, 1988

c) Albertville, 1992

3 Which British figure skater won gold in 1976 at the European Championships, World Championships and Winter Olympics and was also voted BBC Sports Personality of the Year?

a) Chris Howarth

b) John Curry

c) Robin Cousins

4 Which judging system was used to score figure skating performances prior to 2005?

a) The ISU judging system

b) The Olympic scoring system

c) The 6.0 system

5 Which East German figure skater in the 1980s won two Winter Olympic gold medals, four World Championships and six successive European Championships?

a) Anett Pötzsch

b) Katarina Witt

c) Christine Errath

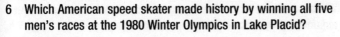

6 Which American speed skater made history by winning all five men's races at the 1980 Winter Olympics in Lake Placid?

a) Peter Mueller

b) Eric Flaim

c) Eric Heiden

7 What sort of ice dance manoeuvres are sit, camel and upright?

a) Spins

b) Jumps

c) Lifts

8 Which American speed skater won five gold medals and one bronze in the Winter Olympics between 1988 and 1994?

a) Jennifer Rodriguez

b) Bonnie Blair

c) Christine Witty

9 At the Winter Olympics, what is the maximum length of a men's speed skating race?

a) 5,000m

b) 10,000m

c) 12,000m

10 Which country won the first nine ice dance gold medals following the launch of the event at the World Figure Skating Championships in 1952?

a) Great Britain

b) USA

c) Canada

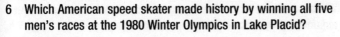
OTHER SPORTS

A

1	a
2	c
3	b
4	c
5	b
6	c
7	a
8	b
9	b
10	a

MARTIAL ARTS

1 Who won four World Judo Championships but missed out on her chance of Olympic success because of injury?

a) Karen Briggs

b) Kate Howey

c) Sharon Rendle

2 Who was the first British judo player to win a medal at the Olympic Games?

a) Neil Eckersley

b) Neil Adams

c) Brian Jacks

3 Which country has won the most Olympic medals for judo?

a) South Korea

b) Cuba

c) Japan

4 Which of the following countries has *not* won a medal for judo at the Olympics?

a) Denmark

b) Iceland

c) Latvia

5 At which Olympics did Sarah Stevenson win Great Britain's first medal for taekwondo?

a) Sydney, 2000

b) Athens, 2004

c) Beijing, 2008

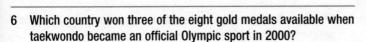

6 Which country won three of the eight gold medals available when taekwondo became an official Olympic sport in 2000?

a) Japan

b) South Korea

c) Taiwan

7 The name of which martial art translates as 'empty hand' in English?

a) Aikido

b) Karate

c) Ju-jitsu

8 Which martial art in addition to karate, wushu and sumo is performed at the World Games for non-Olympic sports?

a) Ju-jitsu

b) Kung fu

c) Aikido

9 With which martial art would you associate Toshio Fujiwara, Peter Cunningham and Rob Kaman?

a) Judo

b) Kickboxing

c) Karate

10 In which martial art is salt thrown into the ring as part of the purification ritual?

a) Kendo

b) Ju-jitsu

c) Sumo

A

1	a
2	c
3	c
4	a
5	c
6	b
7	b
8	a
9	b
10	c

POLO

1   Which London club shares its name with the governing body for polo in the UK and Ireland?

a)   Queen's

b)   Stoke Park

c)   Hurlingham

2   What is the name of the indoor version of polo?

a)   Arena polo

b)   Mini-polo

c)   Rainy-day polo

3   What is the width of the goal in polo?

a)   Eight yards (7.3m)

b)   Twelve yards (11.0m)

c)   Fourteen yards (12.8m)

4   Which member of the royal family broke an arm when they fell while playing polo in 1990?

a)   The Princess Royal

b)   The Duke of Edinburgh

c)   The Prince of Wales

5   What nationality is Marcos Uranga, the first president of the Federation of International Polo?

a)   Chilean

b)   Argentine

c)   Spanish

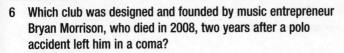

6 Which club was designed and founded by music entrepreneur Bryan Morrison, who died in 2008, two years after a polo accident left him in a coma?

a) Royal County of Berkshire Polo Club

b) Ascot Park Polo Club

c) Rutland Polo Club

7 What is the title of the referee who sits on the sidelines and arbitrates in the event of a disagreement between the two mounted umpires?

a) Arbiter

b) Judge

c) Third man

8 Which actor, whose film credits include *JFK, Men in Black* and *Space Cowboys*, described polo as 'the finest thing a man and a horse can do together'?

a) Will Smith

b) Tommy Lee Jones

c) Kevin Costner

9 What disrupted the 2008 Coronation Cup match between England and Australia?

a) Streakers

b) Animal rights protesters

c) Flooding

10 Which animals are used instead of horses for a variant of polo played in countries such as India, Sri Lanka, Thailand and Nepal?

a) Elephants

b) Llamas

c) Donkeys

A

1	c
2	a
3	a
4	c
5	b
6	a
7	c
8	b
9	a
10	a

ROWING

OTHER SPORTS

1 What was the name of the first woman to take part in the University Boat Race?

a) Sue Brown

b) Liz White

c) Lisa Greene

2 What was remarkable about the 1912 University Boat Race?

a) Oxford sank

b) Cambridge sank

c) Both boats sank

3 What is the length of an international standard rowing course?

a) 1,000m

b) 1,500m

c) 2,000m

4 Which country retains its standing as one of the most successful Olympic rowing nations despite the fact that it has not competed since 1988?

a) Soviet Union

b) East Germany

c) Yugoslavia

5 What nationality is Elisabeta Lipa, who won a total of eight rowing medals, including five golds, at six Olympic Games?

a) German

b) Italian

c) Romanian

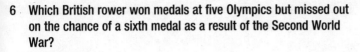

6 Which British rower won medals at five Olympics but missed out on the chance of a sixth medal as a result of the Second World War?

a) Jack Beresford

b) Dick Southwood

c) Peter Jackson

7 Great Britain finished top of the rowing medal table at the 2008 Beijing Olympics, but with how many medals?

a) Four

b) Six

c) Ten

8 Where is Dorney Lake, venue for the rowing events at the 2012 Olympics?

a) Eton

b) Henley-on-Thames

c) Nottingham

9 Who partnered Steve Redgrave to four of his seven wins in the coxless pairs at the Henley Royal Regatta?

a) James Cracknell

b) Andy Holmes

c) Matthew Pinsent

10 In which event at the Henley Royal Regatta do teams compete for the Prince of Wales Challenge Cup?

a) Quadruple sculls

b) Coxed fours

c) Eights

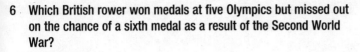

A

1	a
2	c
3	c
4	b
5	c
6	a
7	b
8	a
9	c
10	a

SAILING

1 Which team finished second to Great Britain in the sailing medals table at the 2008 Beijing Olympics?

a) Argentina

b) New Zealand

c) Australia

2 Which British competitor won his third consecutive sailing gold medal at the 2008 Beijing Olympics?

a) Ben Ainslie

b) Iain Percy

c) Andrew Simpson

3 Which country won its only sailing medal in 1980, when David Wilkins and James Wilkinson took silver in the Flying Dutchman class?

a) Netherlands

b) Ireland

c) Bermuda

4 Which British venue hosted the final round of the 2008–9 Sailing World Cup?

a) Eastbourne

b) Weymouth

c) Cowes

5 Which country hosted the inaugural Sailing World Championships in 2003?

a) Australia

b) Portugal

c) Spain

6 Which country took line honours in the Sydney to Hobart yacht race in 1962 with *Ondine*, becoming the first winner from outside Australia since Great Britain won the first race in 1945?

a) USA

b) New Zealand

c) South Africa

7 On which day of the year does the Sydney to Hobart yacht race traditionally start?

a) Boxing Day

b) New Year's Day

c) Australia Day

8 Which Spanish city in 2007 became the first European venue to host the America's Cup since the inaugural race in 1851?

a) Barcelona

b) Valencia

c) Seville

9 What was the name of the yacht that won the America's Cup in 1983, inflicting the first defeat on the USA in the history of the challenge?

a) *Australia*

b) *Australia II*

c) *Kookaburra*

10 From which port did the Clipper Round the World Race set sail in September 2009?

a) La Rochelle

b) Hull

c) Qingdao

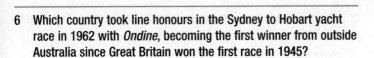

1	c
2	a
3	b
4	b
5	c
6	a
7	a
8	b
9	b
10	b

SNOOKER

1 Which city became home to the World Snooker Championships in 1977?

a) Birmingham

b) Liverpool

c) Sheffield

2 How many balls (not including the cue ball) are used in a game of snooker?

a) 18

b) 21

c) 24

3 Which former world champion was known as 'Hurricane'?

a) Alex Higgins

b) John Higgins

c) Stephen Hendry

4 And who was 'the Whirlwind' – one of the great players who never won a world title?

a) Jimmy White

b) Mark Williams

c) Terry Griffiths

5 Who won the world title on the first 15 occasions that it was contested?

a) Fred Davis

b) Joe Davis

c) Steve Davis

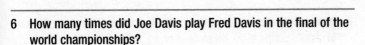

OTHER SPORTS

6 How many times did Joe Davis play Fred Davis in the final of the world championships?

a) None

b) Once

c) Three times

7 What is the nationality of former world champion Cliff Thorburn?

a) Scottish

b) Australian

c) Canadian

8 Who compiled a maximum break in 5 minutes and 20 seconds in the world championships in 1997?

a) Ronnie O'Sullivan

b) Ken Doherty

c) Peter Ebdon

9 Which snooker star was the inspiration for a puppet on the TV series *Spitting Image*?

a) Steve Davis

b) Dennis Taylor

c) John Parrott

10 Which snooker star claimed to drink six pints of beer before a match, and then one pint for every frame, because of a medical condition?

a) Joe Johnson

b) Bill Werbeniuk

c) Kirk Stevens

A

1 c

2 b

3 a

4 a

5 b

6 b

7 c

8 a

9 a

10 b

SQUASH AND TABLE TENNIS

1 What nationality is Geoff Hunt, who won the British Open Squash Championships eight times between 1969 and 1981?

a) American

b) Canadian

c) Australian

2 Which British-based Irishman beat Geoff Hunt in the 1970 and 1972 finals and won the championship six times in his career?

a) Jerry Barrington

b) Joey Barrington

c) Jonah Barrington

3 Which female squash player lost only two matches in her career and was unbeaten from 1962 until her retirement in 1981?

a) Anne Smith

b) Heather McKay

c) Vicki Hoffman

4 Players from which country dominated squash during the 1980s and 1990s, winning 14 out of 16 World Opens between 1981 and 1996?

a) Pakistan

b) India

c) Australia

5 Who was the first British squash player to win the men's World Open in 1999, having lost in the previous two finals?

a) Peter Nicol

b) Peter Marshall

c) Del Harris

6 Which country was the last to win Olympic gold medals in the men's and women's table tennis doubles before the events were replaced by team competitions in 2008?

a) China

b) South Korea

c) Hong Kong

7 Which sport and entertainment agent played table tennis for Great Britain at the 1988 Seoul Olympics in his former career?

a) Imre Varadi

b) Sky Andrew

c) Eric Hall

8 To the nearest centimetre, what is the regulation height of the net in table tennis?

a) 15cm (6in)

b) 18cm (7in)

c) 20cm (8in)

9 Which was the only nation other than China to win the world team table tennis men's championship between 1981 and 2008, with four wins to China's ten?

a) Sweden

b) South Korea

c) Japan

10 Which tennis legend was also a table tennis world champion?

a) Bunny Austin

b) Fred Perry

c) Jean Borotra

A

1	c
2	c
3	b
4	a
5	a
6	a
7	b
8	a
9	a
10	b

SWIMMING

1 Where did the 1912 Olympic swimming events take place?

a) The Stockholm canal

b) Stockholm harbour

c) Lake Malaren

2 What equipment was used for the first time at the 1976 Olympics in Montreal?

a) Goggles

b) Caps

c) Flippers

3 Who was the last woman to win Olympic swimming gold for Great Britain before Rebecca Adlington in 2008?

a) June Croft

b) Sarah Hardcastle

c) Anita Lonsbrough

4 Which British swimmer announced his arrival on the international scene with a bronze medal at the 1970 Commonwealth Games in Edinburgh and crowned his career with gold at the Montreal Olympics in 1976?

a) Paul Naisby

b) David Leigh

c) David Wilkie

5 Which country is top of the all-time Olympic swimming medals table, having won almost three times as many as the second-placed nation?

a) USA

b) Australia

c) Russia

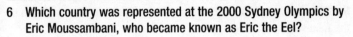

6 Which country was represented at the 2000 Sydney Olympics by Eric Moussambani, who became known as Eric the Eel?

a) Senegal

b) Equatorial Guinea

c) Côte d'Ivoire

7 Which country was represented in the women's 50m freestyle by 12-year-old Antoinette Joyce Guedia Mouafo, the youngest competitor at the 2008 Beijing Games?

a) Cameroon

b) Nigeria

c) Ghana

8 Which British city hosted a Ryder Cup-style swimming challenge – 'The Duel in the Pool' – between Europe and the USA in December 2009?

a) Sheffield

b) Manchester

c) Cardiff

9 In which year were the World Swimming Championships introduced in addition to the World Aquatics Championships?

a) 1993

b) 1995

c) 1997

10 Which event was added to the World Aquatics Championships from 1991?

a) Octopush

b) Synchronised swimming

c) Open water swimming

A

1	b
2	a
3	c
4	c
5	a
6	b
7	a
8	b
9	a
10	c

UNUSUAL SPORTS

Not including substitutes, how many players normally form a team in the following sports?

1 Octopush
a) Six
b) Eight
c) Ten

2 Bandy
a) Seven
b) Eleven
c) Twelve

3 Kabaddi
a) Seven
b) Ten
c) Twelve

4 Handball
a) Five
b) Six
c) Seven

5 Korfball
a) Eight
b) Twelve
c) Sixteen

6 Shinty
a) Seven
b) Ten
c) Twelve

7 Tug of war
a) Eight
b) Ten
c) Twelve

8 Curling
a) Two
b) Three
c) Four

9 Hurling
a) Ten
b) Twelve
c) Fifteen

10 Eton Fives
a) One
b) Two
c) Five

A

1 a

2 b

3 a

4 c

5 a

6 c

7 a

8 c

9 c

10 b

EXTRA TIME

GREAT COMEBACKS

1 Which two players led England's comeback after following-on, to beat Australia at Headingley in the third Ashes Test in 1981?

a) Chris Tavare and Mike Hendrick

b) Mike Gatting and Paul Allott

c) Ian Botham and Bob Willis

2 Who was Liverpool goalkeeper when they recovered from 0–3 to beat AC Milan on penalties in the 2005 Champions League final?

a) Jerzy Dudek

b) Chris Kirkland

c) Jose Reina

3 Who lost the first seven frames of the 1985 world snooker final, but then beat Steve Davis in the 35th and final frame?

a) Dennis Taylor

b) Cliff Thorburn

c) Terry Griffiths

4 Who fell near the halfway mark in the 10,000m at the 1972 Olympics, but recovered to win the race in a world record time?

a) Emiel Puttemans

b) Lasse Viren

c) Kip Keino

5 Which rider lost the first six races of the 2002 World Superbike Championship to Troy Bayliss, but came back with nine straight wins and took the title in the final race?

a) Colin Edwards

b) Makoto Tamada

c) Neil Hodgson

6 Which Formula One driver just missed out on the 1976 world championship after suffering serious injuries in a crash but recovered to win the title the following year?

a) Niki Lauda

b) Carlos Reutemann

c) Jody Scheckter

---

7 Who scored Wembley's first FA Cup final hat-trick in 1953, when Blackpool recovered from 1–3 behind to beat Bolton Wanderers?

a) Stanley Matthews

b) Stan Mortensen

c) Bill Perry

---

8 Which jockey came out of retirement in 1990 and won the Breeders' Cup Mile just short of his 55th birthday?

a) Joe Mercer

b) Lester Piggott

c) Cash Asmussen

---

9 Which player retired from tennis in 1994 aged 37 but returned six years later and won three Grand Slam mixed doubles titles?

a) Hana Mandlikova

b) Martina Navratilova

c) Chris Evert

---

10 Which Yorkshire cricketer – England's youngest player when he made his debut at 18 – became one of England's oldest players when he returned aged 45 to face the West Indies in 1976?

a) Geoff Boycott

b) Ray Illingworth

c) Brian Close

A

1	c
2	a
3	a
4	b
5	a
6	a
7	b
8	b
9	b
10	c

SPORTING RIVALRIES

1 Which sport did Tonya Harding pursue after she was ostracised from figure skating amid allegations of involvement in an attack on rival Nancy Kerrigan?

a) Swimming

b) Cycling

c) Boxing

2 Which American ended the Soviet Union's domination of world chess when he beat Boris Spassky in a high-tension 'best of 21' challenge, held in Iceland in 1972?

a) Bobby Fischer

b) Paul Morphy

c) Robert Byrne

3 What is the record for the longest winning sequence – held by the USA – in golf's fiercest rivalry, the Ryder Cup?

a) Five tournaments

b) Six tournaments

c) Seven tournaments

4 In Argentina, what is the name given to the football derby matches between Boca Juniors and River Plate?

a) Superclasico

b) El Clasico

c) Derby Argentinos

5 At which Olympics did Great Britain's Sebastian Coe and Steve Ovett take their rivalry to a global audience, with Coe taking gold in the 1,500m and Ovett winning the 800m?

a) 1976

b) 1980

c) 1984

6 Which two rugby league sides famously played out their local derby at Wembley for the first time when they met in the Challenge Cup final in 1980?

a) Hull FC and Hull Kingston Rovers

b) Wigan and St Helens

c) Leeds and Bradford

7 What is the name of the trophy awarded to the winners of the annual Six Nations rugby match between England and Scotland?

a) The Six Nations Cup

b) The Anglo-Scottish Cup

c) The Calcutta Cup

8 At which tennis major in 1998 did Venus and Serena Williams first face each other in a professional match?

a) Australian Open

b) French Open

c) Wimbledon

9 Which great cricket rivals met in Canada during the 1990s and in Scotland in 2007 to contest the 'Friendship Cup'?

a) Australia and New Zealand

b) England and Australia

c) India and Pakistan

10 In which stadium do AS Roma meet SS Lazio in their regular Serie A matches?

a) Stadio Artemio Franchi

b) Stadio Olimpico

c) Stadio Delle Alpi

A

1 c

2 a

3 c

4 a

5 b

6 a

7 c

8 a

9 c

10 b

SPORTING INJURIES

1   How did Glenn McGrath sustain the ankle injury that forced him to miss the second Test in the 2005 Ashes series?

a)   He slipped on the pavilion steps

b)   He tripped over the boundary rope

c)   He stood on a cricket ball while playing rugby

2   Which British golfer was forced to withdraw from the 2003 Open because he injured his wrist in a fall on the way to breakfast?

a)   Colin Montgomerie

b)   Paul Lawrie

c)   Nick Faldo

3   Which superstar Chinese athlete limped out of the 2008 Beijing Olympics with Achilles tendon and hamstring injuries?

a)   Meng Yan

b)   Ji Wei

c)   Liu Xiang

4   How did the Cleveland Browns' Orlando Brown sustain a career-threatening eye injury in a match against the Jacksonville Jaguars in 1999?

a)   He was punched by an opposing player

b)   He was struck by a penalty flag thrown by a touch judge

c)   He was struck by a water bottle

5   After a victory against Sheffield Wednesday in the 1993 League Cup final, which Arsenal player broke his collarbone when he was dropped on to the Wembley pitch by Tony Adams?

a)   Steve Morrow

b)   Steve Bould

c)   Martin Keown

6 When doctors operated in 2003 to save the infected arm of Wigan's rugby league player Jamie Ainscough what did they find?

a) A fragment of stud from a boot

b) A tooth from an opposing player

c) A shard of glass

7 When world heavyweight champion Mike Tyson added to his notoriety by biting an opponent's ear, who was the victim?

a) Tony Tubbs

b) Frank Bruno

c) Evander Holyfield

8 What ended the French athlete Salim Sdiri's participation in a Golden League event in Rome in 2007 as he warmed up?

a) He was hit by a javelin

b) He fell into the water jump

c) His vision was impaired by a laser from the crowd

9 Which former FA Cup-winning captain missed the start of the 1993–4 season after dropping a jar of salad cream on his foot?

a) Bryan Robson

b) Gary Mabbutt

c) Dave Beasant

10 What did the England prop Colin Smart drink during a banquet following the 1982 Five Nations win over France that left him needing to have his stomach pumped?

a) Too much beer

b) Aftershave

c) Shampoo

A

1	c
2	a
3	c
4	b
5	a
6	b
7	c
8	a
9	c
10	b

ACCIDENTS, UPSETS AND DISASTERS

1   Which nation pulled off a surprise win in the men's basketball at the 2004 Athens Olympics?

a)   Greece

b)   China

c)   Argentina

2   How did Cuba's Angel Valodia Matos react to being disqualified during a taekwondo bronze medal match at Beijing 2008?

a)   Accepted defeat graciously

b)   Lodged an appeal with the judges

c)   Kicked the referee in the head

3   Who was the manager of AFC Bournemouth when they knocked Manchester United out of the FA Cup in 1984?

a)   Alec Stock

b)   Bobby Gould

c)   Harry Redknapp

4   Which rugby league coach caused Challenge Cup final upsets with Sheffield Eagles against Wigan in 1998 and Hull FC against Leeds Rhinos in 2005?

a)   Brian Smith

b)   John Kear

c)   Steve McNamara

5   Which country was knocked out of the 2003 Cricket World Cup after they miscalculated the runs required to win under the Duckworth-Lewis method?

a)   England

b)   West Indies

c)   South Africa

6 Which boxer was written off by fight fans ahead of his 1990 bout with Mike Tyson but lifted himself off the canvas to win?

a) Riddick Bowe

b) Tony Tucker

c) Buster Douglas

7 Eighth seed Kevin Curren beat Stefan Edberg, John McEnroe and Jimmy Connors on his way to the 1985 Wimbledon final – where he lost to which unseeded teenager?

a) Pat Cash

b) Boris Becker

c) Andre Agassi

8 At which course did Jean Van der Velde famously throw away the 1999 Open Championship as he waded into a stream, recorded a triple bogey on the final hole and then lost the play-off?

a) Carnoustie

b) Royal Troon

c) St Andrews

9 Which nation's men's and women's teams were knocked out of the 4 x 100m at the 2008 Olympics after dropping the baton?

a) Great Britain

b) Jamaica

c) USA

10 In football, which country beat Italy at Middlesbrough in 1966 to cause one of the greatest shocks in World Cup history?

a) North Korea

b) Japan

c) Saudi Arabia

A

1	c
2	c
3	c
4	b
5	c
6	c
7	b
8	a
9	c
10	a

SPORTING FAMILIES

1   Which father and son team won the Grand National as jockey and trainer in 2000?

a)   Ruby and Ted Walsh

b)   Paul and Tommy Carberry

c)   David and Martin Pipe

2   What nationality are Peter and Pavol Hochschorner, who won their third consecutive Olympic gold medal in the canoe slalom at Beijing 2008?

a)   German

b)   Slovakian

c)   Dutch

3   Newcastle United legend Jackie Milburn was related to which footballing brothers?

a)   Les and Dennis Allen

b)   Peter and Ron Springett

c)   Bobby and Jackie Charlton

4   Which member of a famous cricketing family captained England for one Test, against the West Indies at Headingley in 1988?

a)   Ian Greig

b)   Mark Butcher

c)   Chris Cowdrey

5   In which decade did brothers Harold and Arthur Wheatley play for the England rugby union team?

a)   1930s

b)   1950s

c)   1960s

6 Gary Megson has managed West Bromwich Albion and Bolton Wanderers. His father Don was the manager of which two football clubs?

a) Sheffield Wednesday and Rotherham United

b) Coventry City and Walsall

c) AFC Bournemouth and Bristol Rovers

7 Which daughter of a former world heavyweight champion did Laila Ali beat in June 2001?

a) Freeda Foreman

b) Jackie Frazier-Lyde

c) Tracy Byrd

8 Which former England cricketer was followed into the sport by his son who eventually left the game to pursue a rugby career?

a) Ian Botham

b) Mike Gatting

c) Chris Old

9 The brother of which tennis star played baseball with the San Francisco Giants, Houston Astros and Toronto Blue Jays?

a) Billie Jean King

b) Chris Evert

c) Pam Shriver

10 In 2009, in which sport did John and Sinead Kerr win Great Britain's first European championship medal since 1994?

a) Canoeing

b) Squash

c) Ice skating

A

1	a
2	b
3	c
4	c
5	a
6	c
7	b
8	a
9	a
10	c

FAMOUS PARTNERSHIPS

1 In the 1970s, Bruce Bannister and Alan Warboys struck up a lethal strike partnership at Bristol Rovers. What did they become known as?

a) Tip and Tap

b) Smash and Grab

c) Little and Large

2 Who became famous as Muhammad Ali's cornerman throughout his heavyweight boxing career?

a) Al Gavin

b) Don King

c) Angelo Dundee

3 What was the name of the horse ridden by Harry Llewellyn for the Great Britain team that won showjumping gold at the 1952 Helsinki Olympics?

a) Foxhunter

b) Hedgehunter

c) Deerhunter

4 For which English first-class cricket county did Barry Richards and Gordon Greenidge form a fearsome opening batting partnership during the 1970s?

a) Sussex

b) Worcestershire

c) Hampshire

5 Who partnered John McEnroe to success in 57 men's doubles titles including seven majors?

a) Peter Fleming

b) Patrick McEnroe

c) Michael Stich

6 **Which partnership fell out over a mobile phone call during their event at the 2008 Beijing Olympics?**

a) Serena and Venus Williams

b) Usain Bolt and Asafa Powell

c) Tom Daley and Blake Aldridge

7 **Brian Clough and Peter Taylor formed one of football's great managerial partnerships, but which club did they both play for?**

a) Middlesbrough

b) Sunderland

c) Newcastle United

8 **For which golfer did Fanny Sunesson become a famous caddy, helping her employer to win four majors during the 1990s?**

a) Sandy Lyle

b) Nick Faldo

c) Greg Norman

9 **Which TV commentator forged a popular on-screen partnership with Frank Bruno through their post-fight interviews?**

a) Dickie Davies

b) Harry Carpenter

c) Frank Bough

10 **Which British Formula One driver indulged in a high-profile squabble with his team-mate as they challenged for the world championship in 2008?**

a) Lewis Hamilton

b) Jenson Button

c) David Coulthard

A

1	b
2	c
3	a
4	c
5	a
6	c
7	a
8	b
9	b
10	a

NICKNAMES

1   Which football club are known as 'the Brewers'?

a)   Burton Albion

b)   Notts County

c)   Chesterfield

2   Which West Indies fast bowler was known as 'Whispering Death'?

a)   Andy Roberts

b)   Joel Garner

c)   Michael Holding

3   What nickname was bestowed on rugby star Martin Offiah because of his blistering pace?

a)   The Wigan Flyer

b)   Chariots

c)   Wildfire

4   Which 1980s American footballer was known as 'the Refrigerator' because of his size?

a)   William Perry

b)   Randy White

c)   Richard Dent

5   Which former Real Madrid star was fondly known as 'the Galloping Major'?

a)   Luis Figo

b)   Ferenc Puskas

c)   Emilio Butragueno

6 Which snooker star is known as 'the Rocket'?

a) Ray Reardon

b) Ronnie O'Sullivan

c) Steve Davis

7 Which name did Shirley Crabtree adopt during his successful wrestling career?

a) Dynamite Kid

b) Giant Haystacks

c) Big Daddy

8 Which legendary boxer was known as 'the Louisville Lip'?

a) Muhammad Ali

b) Joe Louis

c) Sonny Liston

9 Which golfer became known as 'the Walrus'?

a) Sam Torrance

b) Craig Stadler

c) Brad Bryant

10 Why was former England cricketer Phil Tufnell known as 'the Cat'?

a) Because he liked cats

b) Because of his agility in the field

c) Because he slept a lot

A

1 a

2 c

3 b

4 a

5 b

6 b

7 c

8 a

9 b

10 c

TROPHIES AND AWARDS

In which sports are the following cups or trophies awarded?

1 Lance Todd Trophy
a) Cycling
b) Cricket
c) Rugby league

2 Sam Maguire Cup
a) Gaelic football
b) Hurling
c) Horse racing

3 Kinnaird Cup
a) Eton Fives
b) Rugby Fives
c) Football

4 Henri Delaunay Cup
a) Polo
b) Tennis
c) Football

5 Bledisloe Cup
a) Rugby union
b) Rugby league
c) Australian rules football

6 Stanley Cup
a) Yachting
b) Table tennis
c) Ice hockey

7 Leonard Trophy
a) Squash
b) Shooting
c) Bowls

8 Walker Cup
a) Golf
b) Angling
c) Yachting

9 Vince Lombardi Trophy
a) American football
b) Golf
c) Baseball

10 Giuseppe Garibaldi Trophy
a) Basketball
b) Rugby union
c) Lacrosse

A
1 c
2 a
3 a
4 c
5 a
6 c
7 c
8 a
9 a
10 b

THE FORTIES
THE FIFTIES
THE SIXTIES
THE SEVENTIES
THE EIGHTIES
THE NINETIES
THE NOUGHTIES

HISTORY

THE FORTIES

1 As he lay dying in a German hospital bed in 1943, having been shot and captured in Sicily, who reportedly said: "I think I have played my last innings for Yorkshire"?

a) Hedley Verity

b) Norman Yardley

c) Herbert Sutcliffe

2 During the Second World War baseball players serving in the US army and navy competed in the 'Pacific Service World Series'. Where was it held?

a) Texas

b) Florida

c) Hawaii

3 Which major golf championship was played annually during the Second World War except in 1943?

a) US PGA Championship

b) US Open

c) US Masters

4 Which horse in 1946 won the first postwar Grand National?

a) Russian Hero

b) Lovely Cottage

c) Sheila's Cottage

5 In which events did Great Britain win two gold medals at the 1948 Olympic Games in London?

a) Rowing

b) Sailing

c) Swimming

6 **Which tennis legend of the 1950s and 1960s won his only two Grand Slam tournaments in 1948 and 1949?**

a) Jack Kramer

b) Frank Sedgman

c) Pancho Gonzales

7 **In the 1946–7 season, who became the first postwar champions of the Football League?**

a) Liverpool

b) Arsenal

c) Portsmouth

8 **Which country toured England for a three-match series when Test cricket resumed in 1946 after the war?**

a) Australia

b) India

c) New Zealand

9 **Which country won their first Grand Slam in the 1948 Five Nations rugby championship?**

a) Ireland

b) Scotland

c) Wales

10 **In March 1949, at the age of 51, Neil McBain became the oldest man ever to play in the Football League. Who did he play for?**

a) Newport County

b) Newcastle United

c) New Brighton

A

1	a
2	c
3	a
4	b
5	a
6	c
7	a
8	b
9	a
10	c

THE FIFTIES

1 Which country won the Five Nations Grand Slam in 1950 and again in 1952?

a) France

b) England

c) Wales

2 In 1953 England's football team suffered their first-ever home defeat to continental opposition. Who were the victorious opponents?

a) Italy

b) Czechoslovakia

c) Hungary

3 Which Australian tennis star won three of his four career Grand Slam events in 1956?

a) Lew Hoad

b) Ken Rosewall

c) Ashley Cooper

4 Which country won their first Test cricket series on English soil in the summer of 1950?

a) New Zealand

b) South Africa

c) West Indies

5 Which event's semi-finals at the 1956 Olympics ended in bloodshed when competitors from the Soviet Union and Hungary clashed over political unrest?

a) Football

b) Boxing

c) Water polo

6 What nationality was Juan Manuel Fangio, who won four Formula One world drivers' titles in the 1950s?

a) Brazilian

b) Argentine

c) Spanish

7 Who secured the first of his nine major golf championships when he won the Open at Muirfield in 1959?

a) Arnold Palmer

b) Gary Player

c) Peter Thomson

8 Who in 1958 became the first British competitor to win the Formula One World Drivers' Championship?

a) Mike Hawthorn

b) John Surtees

c) Stirling Moss

9 Which trainer achieved a hat-trick of Grand National wins with three different horses from 1953 to 1955?

a) Fred Winter

b) Vincent O'Brien

c) Neville Crump

10 Which national cricket team played its first-ever Test match in 1952?

a) Bangladesh

b) Sri Lanka

c) Pakistan

A

1	c
2	c
3	a
4	c
5	c
6	b
7	b
8	a
9	b
10	c

THE SIXTIES

---

1   Besides Ipswich Town, which football club won the First Division title for the first time during the 1960s?

a)   Burnley

b)   Leeds United

c)   Manchester City

---

2   Which tennis player won 11 major titles during the 1960s including the Grand Slam in 1962 and 1969?

a)   John Newcombe

b)   Roy Emerson

c)   Rod Laver

---

3   Which American city hosted the first Super Bowl in 1967?

a)   Dallas

b)   Los Angeles

c)   New York

---

4   Who won the light heavyweight boxing gold medal at the 1960 Olympic Games?

a)   Daniel Bekker

b)   Wilbert McClure

c)   Cassius Clay

---

5   Which 100-1 outsider won the 1967 Grand National after most of the other horses fell?

a)   Foinavon

b)   Devon Loch

c)   Red Alligator

6 What was the name of the first limited-overs cricket competition, introduced in England in 1963?

a) Lord's Taverners Challenge

b) Gillette Cup

c) Schweppes Cup

7 Which of the home rugby union nations shared a 0–0 draw with the All Blacks during their 1963–4 tour of the northern hemisphere?

a) Scotland

b) Wales

c) Ireland

8 Which rugby league player famously missed a last-minute kick at goal, denying Wakefield Trinity victory in the final of the 1968 Challenge Cup?

a) Neil Fox

b) Don Fox

c) Ken Hirst

9 Name the event where Dick Fosbury won gold at the 1968 Olympics with his 'flop' technique?

a) Triple jump

b) High jump

c) Pole vault

10 During the 1966 World Cup in England, who was the manager of West Germany?

a) Helmut Schön

b) Uwe Seeler

c) Jupp Derwall

A

1	b
2	c
3	b
4	c
5	a
6	b
7	a
8	b
9	b
10	a

THE SEVENTIES

1 **Which player won the men's singles at Wimbledon in 1973, when a number of top players boycotted the tournament?**

a) Stan Smith

b) Jan Kodes

c) Alex Metreveli

2 **After the proposed tour by the official South Africa cricket team was cancelled, how many South African cricketers joined a Rest of the World side for a 1970 tour of England?**

a) Three

b) Four

c) Five

3 **In 1977 Don Revie resigned as manager of England to take charge of which national football team?**

a) Qatar

b) Oman

c) United Arab Emirates

4 **Which event was dropped from the Motorcycle Grand Prix World Championship after the 1976 round of races?**

a) British Grand Prix

b) South African Grand Prix

c) Isle of Man TT (Tourist Trophy)

5 **Which horse in 1970 won the Triple Crown of the 2,000 Guineas, the Derby and the St Leger?**

a) Alleged

b) Nijinsky

c) Mill Reef

6 Who was sent off along with Leeds United's Billy Bremner during the 1974 FA Charity Shield match at Wembley?

a) Ron Harris

b) Kevin Keegan

c) Norman Hunter

7 Which cyclist won the Tour de France four times during the 1970s?

a) Eddy Merckx

b) Bernard Hinault

c) Greg LeMond

8 Which country in 1974 hosted the showdown between Muhammad Ali and George Foreman known as the 'Rumble in the Jungle'?

a) Nigeria

b) Zaire

c) Brazil

9 Who was the only female competitor at the 1976 Olympic Games to be excused a sex test?

a) Renate Stecher

b) Princess Anne

c) Nadia Comaneci

10 Who was the last player to beat Bjorn Borg at Wimbledon in the 1970s, in the 1975 quarter-final?

a) Manuel Orantes

b) Guillermo Vilas

c) Arthur Ashe

A

1	b
2	c
3	c
4	c
5	b
6	b
7	a
8	b
9	b
10	c

THE EIGHTIES

---

1 What was the name of the alternative competition organised in Philadelphia for countries that boycotted the 1980 Olympics in Moscow?

a) The Alternative Games

b) The Freedom Games

c) The Liberty Bell Classic

---

2 What was the name of the alternative competition organised at various venues for countries that boycotted the 1984 Olympics in Los Angeles?

a) The Friendship Games

b) The Solidarity Games

c) The Peace Games

---

3 Who became the youngest winner of a tennis Grand Slam singles title when he won the 1989 French Open at the age of 17?

a) Yannick Noah

b) Mats Wilander

c) Michael Chang

---

4 Which Football League club imposed a ban on away supporters in 1986?

a) Oldham Athletic

b) Luton Town

c) Swansea City

---

5 In 1982 which player captained a rebel tour of South Africa by 15 of England's top cricket players?

a) Graham Gooch

b) Geoff Boycott

c) Bob Woolmer

6 **Which horse became the first to win the Grand National with a female trainer in 1983?**

a) Corbiere

b) Hallo Dandy

c) West Tip

---

7 **Which country won the inaugural Rugby World Cup in 1987?**

a) Australia

b) England

c) New Zealand

---

8 **Which city had at least one team competing in six of the ten rugby league Challenge Cup finals contested during the 1980s?**

a) Leeds

b) Hull

c) Bradford

---

9 **Which former European Footballer of the Year was signed by Charlton Athletic in 1982?**

a) Allan Simonsen

b) Oleg Blokhin

c) Gianni Rivera

---

10 **Which sprinter set a world record for the men's 100m at the 1988 Olympics but was subsequently disqualified after the detection of a banned substance?**

a) Calvin Smith

b) Ben Johnson

c) Linford Christie

A

1	c
2	a
3	c
4	b
5	a
6	a
7	c
8	b
9	a
10	b

THE NINETIES

---

1   Who was the leading scorer of the Euro 96 tournament in England?

a)   Alan Shearer

b)   Jürgen Klinsmann

c)   Davor Suker

---

2   Which tennis player won the last of her 22 Grand Slam singles titles at the 1999 French Open?

a)   Martina Navratilova

b)   Steffi Graf

c)   Chris Evert

---

3   Who scored 100 in each innings in 1994 when England inflicted defeat on the West Indies in Barbados?

a)   Mike Atherton

b)   Robin Smith

c)   Alec Stewart

---

4   Who won the 1992 Formula One World Drivers' Championship with five races to spare and finished with a record margin of 52 points?

a)   Alain Prost

b)   Nigel Mansell

c)   Michael Schumacher

---

5   Which team in 1999 became the first from outside the rugby league's northern heartland to reach the final of the Challenge Cup?

a)   Paris Saint-Germain

b)   Celtic Crusaders

c)   London Broncos

6 Who wrote and performed on a song that became the theme for the 1992 Olympic Games in Barcelona?

a) Freddie Mercury

b) Paul McCartney

c) Phil Collins

7 Which club finished bottom of the Premier League at the end of its first season in 1993?

a) Queens Park Rangers

b) Nottingham Forest

c) Coventry City

8 How many Grand Slam singles did Pete Sampras win during the 1990s?

a) Eight

b) Ten

c) Twelve

9 Who became the first bowler to take 400 Test wickets in his career in 1990?

a) Richard Hadlee

b) Imran Khan

c) Courtney Walsh

10 Which golfer won the most majors during the 1990s?

a) Payne Stewart

b) Nick Faldo

c) Tiger Woods

A

1	a
2	b
3	c
4	b
5	c
6	a
7	b
8	c
9	a
10	b

THE NOUGHTIES

Who were the first winners of the following events in the Noughties?

1 FA Cup
a) Liverpool
b) Manchester United
c) Chelsea

2 Six Nations
a) England
b) France
c) Wales

3 Olympic Games: men's 100m
a) Donovan Bailey
b) Tim Montgomery
c) Maurice Green

4 Super Bowl
a) St Louis Rams
b) Green Bay Packers
c) New England Patriots

5 Grand National
a) Papillon
b) Bobbyjo
c) Monty's Pass

6 Cricket World Cup
a) India
b) Australia
c) West Indies

7 Rugby League World Cup
a) New Zealand
b) Australia
c) Great Britain

8 Rugby Union World Cup
a) South Africa
b) France
c) England

9 World Athletics Championships: men's triple jump
a) Christian Olsson
b) Jonathan Edwards
c) Charles Friedek

10 America's Cup
a) Team New Zealand
b) Australia II
c) Stars & Stripes

A

1 c
2 a
3 c
4 a
5 a
6 b
7 b
8 c
9 b
10 a

★ EASY

★ ★ MEDIUM

★ ★ ★ HARD

GENERAL KNOWLEDGE

EASY – PART 1

GENERAL KNOWLEDGE

1 Where were the 2006 Commonwealth Games held?

a) Melbourne

b) Manchester

c) Ontario

2 Which British football team won the 1967 European Cup?

a) Manchester United

b) Celtic

c) Arsenal

3 What substance are the beds of good snooker tables made from?

a) Pine

b) Slate

c) Oak

4 What is the name of Arsenal's home ground?

a) Gulf Stadium

b) Dubai Stadium

c) Emirates Stadium

5 In snooker, what colour ball is worth four points?

a) Brown

b) Yellow

c) Purple

6 Where was former England cricket captain Nasser Hussain born?

a) India

b) Wales

c) Australia

7 Which cricket ground is the headquarters of the MCC?

a) The Oval

b) Lord's

c) Riverside

8 How many furlongs are there in a mile?

a) Eight

b) Ten

c) Twelve

9 Which nation's rugby players perform the haka before matches?

a) New Zealand

b) France

c) Argentina

10 Which English seaside resort is the home to a famous pre-Wimbledon ladies' tennis tournament?

a) Scarborough

b) Blackpool

c) Eastbourne

A

1 a

2 b

3 b

4 c

5 a

6 a

7 b

8 a

9 a

10 c

EASY – PART 2

1 Which football club play their home matches at Fratton Park?

a) Port Vale

b) Portsmouth

c) Preston North End

2 What nationality is the England cricketer Eoin Morgan?

a) Irish

b) Scottish

c) Zimbabwean

3 Which rugby league team changed its name from Northern to the Bulls with the introduction of the Super League?

a) Batley

b) Bradford

c) Bingley

4 Which snooker star opted out of the 2009 UK championships and instead entered the reality TV show *I'm a Celebrity… Get Me Out of Here*?

a) Jimmy White

b) Stephen Hendry

c) Steve Davis

5 Who was Alex Ferguson's predecessor as manager of Manchester United?

a) Ron Atkinson

b) Frank O'Farrell

c) Lou Macari

6 Who was named IAAF World Athlete of the Year in both 2008 and 2009?

a) Phillips Idowu

b) Usain Bolt

c) Asafa Powell

7 With which team did Jenson Button win the 2009 Formula One World Drivers' Championship?

a) Brawn GP

b) McLaren

c) Red Bull Racing

8 Where on a cricket field does an umpire stand when the bowling is not from his end of the pitch?

a) Long leg

b) Short leg

c) Square leg

9 What sort of shots are woods used for in golf?

a) Long shots

b) Bunker shots

c) Putting

10 What was the England rugby team's controversial choice of shirt colour for the 2009 autumn international against Argentina?

a) Pink

b) Purple

c) Black

A

1 b
2 a
3 b
4 a
5 a
6 b
7 a
8 c
9 a
10 b

EASY – PART 3

1 Which county released the former England cricketer Matthew Hoggard at the end of the 2009 season?

a) Yorkshire

b) Lancashire

c) Leicestershire

2 While Wembley was being rebuilt between 2001 and 2006, where were FA Cup finals staged?

a) Old Trafford

b) Twickenham

c) Millennium Stadium

3 Which TV commentator became known as the voice of Formula One?

a) Steve Cram

b) Frank Bough

c) Murray Walker

4 Which city hosted the first modern Olympics in 1896?

a) Athens

b) London

c) Paris

5 What position is normally played by a rugby union player wearing the number 15 shirt?

a) Full-back

b) Prop

c) Wing

6 Traditionally, what is the design of Queens Park Rangers' home shirts?

a) Blue and white stripes

b) Blue and white hoops

c) Blue and white halves

7 Which baseball team has recorded the most wins in the World Series?

a) San Francisco Giants

b) Los Angeles Dodgers

c) New York Yankees

8 Which court at Wimbledon has a retractable roof?

a) Court 14

b) No. 1 Court

c) Centre Court

9 Which golfer has won the most major tournaments?

a) Gary Player

b) Jack Nicklaus

c) Nick Faldo

10 The boxer Amir Khan comes from which Lancashire town?

a) Bolton

b) Preston

c) Blackburn

A

1	a
2	c
3	c
4	a
5	a
6	b
7	c
8	c
9	b
10	a

EASY – PART 4

1 Which piece of kit did the Ethiopian Abebe Bikila do without when winning Olympic marathon gold in Rome in 1960?

a) Vest

b) Shorts

c) Shoes

2 What term is used for the start of an ice hockey match?

a) Face-off

b) Kick-off

c) Bully-off

3 Which rugby league team plays its home games at Headingley stadium?

a) Hull FC

b) Leeds Rhinos

c) Wakefield Trinity Wildcats

4 Which football club is nicknamed 'the Toffees'?

a) Everton

b) Wolverhampton Wanderers

c) Stoke City

5 What is the maximum a player can score with three darts?

a) 120

b) 150

c) 180

6 For which first-class cricket county did Graham Gooch score more than 67,000 runs?

a) Sussex

b) Essex

c) Middlesex

7 In which country was the former British number one tennis player Greg Rusedski born?

a) Canada

b) New Zealand

c) Ireland

8 To which football club were Bobby Moore, Geoff Hurst and Martin Peters contracted when they won the 1966 World Cup as members of the England team?

a) Tottenham Hotspur

b) Fulham

c) West Ham United

9 In which sport are the most popular forms freestyle and Greco-Roman?

a) Wrestling

b) Swimming

c) Gymnastics

10 What kind of animal was Sam, the mascot for the 1984 Los Angeles Olympics?

a) A bear

b) An eagle

c) A dolphin

A

1	c
2	a
3	b
4	a
5	c
6	b
7	a
8	c
9	a
10	b

EASY – PART 5

1 Who was the manager of Ipswich Town when they won the FA Cup in 1978?

a) Alf Ramsey

b) Bobby Robson

c) John Lyall

2 Which was the first Asian city to host the Summer Olympics?

a) Tokyo

b) Beijing

c) Seoul

3 How many points is a drop goal worth in rugby league?

a) One

b) Two

c) Three

4 On which score – unlucky in cricket – would the late cricket umpire David Shepherd lift one foot off the ground?

a) 13

b) 111

c) 113

5 What is the name of the diving position in which the body is bent at the waist with the legs straight and the toes pointed?

a) The pike

b) The tuck

c) The twist

6 In American football what position did Dan Marino, John Elway and Brett Favre play?

a) Offensive lineman

b) Wide receiver

c) Quarterback

7 In hockey what shape is the shooting area?

a) Rectangle

b) Semi-circle

c) Triangle

8 In 2003 which football team moved into the stadium that had been used for the 2002 Commonwealth Games?

a) Everton

b) Manchester City

c) Wigan Athletic

9 What is the name of the women's equivalent of the Ryder Cup?

a) The Walker Cup

b) The Solheim Cup

c) The Women's Ryder Cup

10 In cycling, what is 'granny gear'?

a) A low gear

b) A high gear

c) Old-fashioned clothing

A	
1	b
2	a
3	a
4	b
5	a
6	c
7	b
8	b
9	b
10	a

EASY – PART 6

1 Which national football team did the goalkeeper Pat Jennings play for?

a) Republic of Ireland

b) Wales

c) Northern Ireland

2 Which piece of music did Jayne Torvill and Christopher Dean use in winning Olympic gold in 1984?

a) Boléro

b) Miroirs

c) Sonatine

3 How many laps of an athletics track are completed in the 10,000m?

a) 20

b) 25

c) 27

4 According to legend, what sport was Sir Francis Drake playing as the Spanish Armada approached in 1588?

a) Real tennis

b) Bowls

c) Croquet

5 By what nickname did the cricket umpire Harold Bird become known?

a) Dickie

b) Sparrow

c) Chirpy

6 **With which football club did Alan Shearer win the Premier League?**

a) Newcastle United

b) Southampton

c) Blackburn Rovers

7 **Which venue off the English coast is the home of the world's longest-running regular sailing regatta?**

a) Isle of Man

b) Cowes

c) Anglesey

8 **In which sport did an annual tournament increase from four teams to five in 1910 and from five teams to six in 2000?**

a) Tennis

b) Rugby union

c) Football

9 **Which former champion jockey was known as the 'the Long Fellow' on account of his height?**

a) Lester Piggott

b) Willie Carson

c) Frankie Dettori

10 **Which sport is governed by the Queensberry rules?**

a) Tennis

b) Swimming

c) Boxing

A

1	c
2	a
3	b
4	b
5	a
6	c
7	b
8	b
9	a
10	c

EASY – PART 7

1   Which US city hosted the 1984 Summer Olympic Games that were boycotted by 14 countries?

a)   New York

b)   Los Angeles

c)   Atlanta

2   With which aspect of sport would you associate WADA?

a)   Drug testing

b)   Racial equality

c)   Media accreditation

3   Which football club plays its home games at Vicarage Road?

a)   Hartlepool United

b)   Watford

c)   Peterborough United

4   In which sport does the bat have a maximum length of 460mm (18in)?

a)   Rounders

b)   Softball

c)   Baseball

5   Which rugby union team plays its home games at the Stoop?

a)   Leeds

b)   Bath

c)   Harlequins

6 With which first-class cricket county did Monty Panesar begin his career?

a) Derbyshire

b) Leicestershire

c) Northamptonshire

7 Which athlete won the men's 100m in the first three World Athletics championships in 1983, 1987 and 1991?

a) Carl Lewis

b) Leroy Burrell

c) Frankie Fredericks

8 Which island became the home of motorcycle road racing in the early 1900s when racing was banned on mainland Britain?

a) Isle of Skye

b) Isle of Man

c) Isle of Wight

9 Who won the Wimbledon Men's Singles tennis title seven times out of eight from 1993 to 2000?

a) Pete Sampras

b) John McEnroe

c) Andre Agassi

10 What nationality is former football referee Pierluigi Collina?

a) French

b) Greek

c) Italian

A

1 b

2 a

3 b

4 a

5 c

6 c

7 a

8 b

9 a

10 c

EASY – PART 8

1 Who in 2004 became the oldest woman to win Olympic gold at 800m and 1,500m?

a) Joanne Pavey

b) Joanne Fenn

c) Kelly Holmes

2 In cricket, under law 27 what must a fielding side do before a batsman can be given out?

a) Appeal

b) Break the wicket

c) Catch the ball

3 At which golf course would you find the headquarters of the Royal and Ancient Golf Club?

a) St Andrews

b) The Belfry

c) Wentworth

4 Which team led 3–0 before losing the Champions League final to Liverpool in 2005?

a) Rangers

b) AC Milan

c) Real Madrid

5 Which English racecourse is the home of the annual National Hunt festival in March?

a) Newbury

b) Aintree

c) Cheltenham

6 **What colour is the centre scoring zone of an archery target?**

a) Gold

b) Silver

c) Bronze

7 **Which motor racing circuit was set to agree a deal to host the British Formula One Grand Prix from 2010 until Silverstone stepped in?**

a) Brands Hatch

b) Donington Park

c) Brooklands

8 **In netball which player wears the abbreviation GS?**

a) Goal stopper

b) Goal saver

c) Goal shooter

9 **Along with Belgium, which nation staged the Euro 2000 football championship?**

a) Netherlands

b) Luxembourg

c) France

10 **Why are match officials in American football known as zebras?**

a) Sponsor requirements

b) They wear striped shirts

c) It was the nickname of a famous umpire

A

1	c
2	a
3	a
4	b
5	c
6	a
7	b
8	c
9	a
10	b

EASY – PART 9

1 Who replaced Juande Ramos as manager of Tottenham Hotspur in 2008?

a) Glenn Hoddle

b) Harry Redknapp

c) Martin Jol

---

2 Which Winter Olympics featured a unified German team for the first time in 28 years?

a) 1984

b) 1988

c) 1992

---

3 What is the name of the area where the pitcher stands in baseball?

a) The hill

b) The hump

c) The mound

---

4 At which English Test cricket ground would you find the Radcliffe Road End?

a) Edgbaston

b) Trent Bridge

c) The Oval

---

5 What nationality was Ivan Lendl, winner of the men's singles at the French Open in 1984, 1986 and 1987 before he gained US citizenship?

a) German

b) Czech

c) Italian

6   In which sport can you 'catch a crab'?

a)   Rowing

b)   Basketball

c)   Swimming

7   What award is bestowed on the player of the season in rugby's Super League?

a)   Superman

b)   Man of Steel

c)   Most Valuable Player

8   Which British runner set a women's world record in the London Marathon in April 2003?

a)   Paula Radcliffe

b)   Liz McColgan

c)   Mara Yamauchi

9   In which competition did Middlesbrough win their first major trophy in 2004?

a)   Europa League

b)   FA Cup

c)   Carling Cup

10 What term is used to describe a boxer who leads with his right hand?

a)   Southpaw

b)   Orthodox

c)   Slugger

A	
1	b
2	c
3	c
4	b
5	b
6	a
7	b
8	a
9	c
10	a

EASY – PART 10

1 Which Paralympian was the first woman to break the one-minute barrier for the 400m wheelchair race?

a) Tanni Grey-Thompson

b) Sharon Bolton

c) Tracey Hinton

2 In cricket, what term is given to an over in which no runs are scored?

a) Dead rubber

b) No-balls

c) Maiden

3 Which member of the British Royal family competed in the 1976 Olympic Games?

a) Princess Anne

b) Prince Charles

c) The Duke of Kent

4 Which legendary cricket figure was also president of the English Bowls Association?

a) Ian Botham

b) Geoff Boycott

c) W. G. Grace

5 From what material is the sword traditionally made in kendo, the Japanese martial art?

a) Oak

b) Bamboo

c) Willow

6 **Which football team won only one of their Premier League games in the 2007–8 season?**

a) Birmingham City

b) West Ham United

c) Derby County

7 **Who announced in 2009 that he would not be standing for re-election as president of Formula One's governing body?**

a) Max Mosley

b) Bernie Ecclestone

c) Flavio Briatore

8 **Prior to Andy Murray in 2009, in which decade did a British player last win the Queen's Club tennis tournament?**

a) 1930s

b) 1980s

c) 1990s

9 **Which European football competition was discontinued after the 1998–9 season, with teams competing instead in an expanded UEFA Cup?**

a) Intertoto Cup

b) Cup Winners' Cup

c) Inter-Cities Fairs Cup

10 Over how many holes is a major golf tournament contested?

a) 18

b) 36

c) 72

A

1	a
2	c
3	a
4	c
5	b
6	c
7	a
8	a
9	b
10	c

MEDIUM – PART 1

---

1   At which Olympic Games did Steve Redgrave win his first gold medal?

a)   Los Angeles, 1984

b)   Seoul, 1988

c)   Barcelona, 1992

---

2   What was memorable about the 1993 Grand National?

a)   Abandoned because of flooding

b)   Abandoned after two false starts

c)   Two horses tied in a dead heat

---

3   Who was the first professional footballer to be knighted?

a)   Alf Ramsey

b)   Stanley Matthews

c)   Bobby Robson

---

4   What is the points value of a maximum break in snooker?

a)   125

b)   147

c)   201

---

5   In which year did Arsenal move from their Highbury home?

a)   2005

b)   2006

c)   2007

6   Where were the 2006 Winter Olympics held?

a)   Turin

b)   Calgary

c)   Vienna

7   What sport would you be watching if you saw a madison or a pursuit?

a)   Kayaking

b)   Judo

c)   Cycling

8   Who played the part of the boxer Jake La Motta in the 1980 film *Raging Bull*?

a)   Paul Newman

b)   Robert Duvall

c)   Robert De Niro

9   Who co-presented a well-known ITV football chat show with Jimmy Greaves?

a)   Ian St John

b)   Rodney Marsh

c)   Frank Worthington

10 Which former England wicket keeper is also a well-known artist?

a)   Alan Knott

b)   Alec Stewart

c)   Jack Russell

A	
1	a
2	b
3	b
4	b
5	b
6	a
7	c
8	c
9	a
10	c

MEDIUM – PART 2

1   Which football club play their home games at the Pirelli Stadium?

a)   Aldershot Town

b)   Burton Albion

c)   Accrington Stanley

2   Which player captained the England cricket team for the first time in a Twenty20 international in South Africa in November 2009?

a)   Alastair Cook

b)   Kevin Pietersen

c)   Owais Shah

3   What symbol of everyday London life featured in the closing ceremony of the 2008 Beijing Olympics?

a)   A tube train

b)   A telephone box

c)   A double-decker bus

4   Which sport uses stones and a house?

a)   Hurling

b)   Shinty

c)   Curling

5   How much weight did David Haye concede to Nikolai Valuev when beating him to win the WBA heavyweight title in November 2009?

a)   12lbs (5.4kg)

b)   3st (19kg)

c)   7st (44.5kg)

6 Who was the first boxer to become BBC Sports Personality of the Year?

a) Henry Cooper

b) Joe Bugner

c) Muhammad Ali

7 Who was Jim Magilton's predecessor as manager of Queens Park Rangers?

a) Paulo Sousa

b) Luigi De Canio

c) Iain Dowie

8 Which American football team are known as the Seahawks?

a) San Diego

b) Seattle

c) San Francisco

9 Which extreme sport has its origins in a coming-of-age ritual on Pentecost Island?

a) Bungee jumping

b) Wave jumping

c) Hang gliding

10 Which Irish rugby player made his 100th Test appearance in the draw against Australia in November 2009?

a) Gordon D'Arcy

b) Ronan O'Gara

c) Brian O'Driscoll

A

1	b
2	a
3	c
4	c
5	c
6	a
7	a
8	b
9	a
10	c

MEDIUM – PART 3

---

1 Which Caribbean island does Sir Viv Richards come from?

a) Jamaica

b) Barbados

c) Antigua

---

2 Which American athlete broke three world records and equalled a fourth in 1935, a year before dominating the Berlin Olympics?

a) Forrest Towns

b) Archie Williams

c) Jesse Owens

---

3 Which football ground staged the FA Cup final replay between Chelsea and Leeds United in 1970?

a) Wembley

b) Villa Park

c) Old Trafford

---

4 In which sport do the playing positions include forward pockets, rovers and back pockets?

a) Gaelic football

b) Australian football

c) American football

---

5 Which player kicked the winning drop goal when England won the Rugby World Cup in 2003?

a) Matt Dawson

b) Jason Robinson

c) Jonny Wilkinson

6 **Who did Kevin Pietersen replace as England's one-day cricket captain in 2008?**

a) Paul Collingwood

b) Michael Vaughan

c) Andrew Strauss

7 **What are the traditional colours of the stripes on Hull City's football shirts?**

a) Black and white

b) Black and amber

c) Claret and amber

8 **Which rugby league team won the Challenge Cup for the third consecutive year in 2008?**

a) Wigan Warriors

b) St Helens

c) Warrington Wolves

9 **Which athlete won a 150m street race in Manchester in May 2009?**

a) Usain Bolt

b) Marlon Devonish

c) Mark Lewis-Francis

10 **Who took fourth place in the 2009 Tour de France to equal the best-ever finish by a British cyclist?**

a) Mark Cavendish

b) Bradley Wiggins

c) Sir Chris Hoy

MEDIUM – PART 4

1   Which country won the 2009 rugby league Four Nations tournament?

a)   Australia

b)   England

c)   New Zealand

2   What items were allegedly thrown on to the field by England's cricketers to the annoyance of India's Zaheer Khan during the second Test at Trent Bridge in 2007?

a)   Stones

b)   Coins

c)   Jelly beans

3   What sort of animal was Waldi, the official mascot at the Munich Olympics in 1972?

a)   A dog

b)   A bear

c)   A squirrel

4   How many innings are normally played in a game of softball?

a)   Seven

b)   Eight

c)   Nine

5   Which former Football League club is known as 'the Seadogs'?

a)   Southport

b)   Scarborough

c)   Chester

6 How much higher is a men's sprint hurdle (to the nearest cm) than the version used in the 400m?

a) 13cm (five inches)

b) 15cm (six inches)

c) 20cm (eight inches)

7 Which team did Ireland beat in the final match of the 2009 Six Nations tournament to complete the Grand Slam?

a) England

b) Wales

c) France

8 Which London-based football team became known as 'the Crazy Gang' during the 1980s?

a) Chelsea

b) Brentford

c) Wimbledon

9 Who was named British Athlete of the Year for 2008 by the British Olympic Association?

a) Christine Ohuruogu

b) Germaine Mason

c) Phillips Idowu

10 Which Caribbean island hosted the 2008 challenge between the England cricket team and the Stanford Superstars?

a) Antigua

b) Trinidad

c) St Lucia

A

1 a

2 c

3 a

4 a

5 b

6 b

7 b

8 c

9 a

10 a

MEDIUM – PART 5

1   Who was the manager of Wimbledon when they won the FA Cup in 1988?

a)   Dave Bassett

b)   Egil Olsen

c)   Bobby Gould

2   How did long jumper Jade Johnson sustain an injury in 2009 that hindered her winter training plans?

a)   Tripped over her cat

b)   Practising for *Strictly Come Dancing*

c)   Running for a taxi

3   Who beat the Russian favourite Yuri Kutsenko to win decathlon gold at the 1980 Moscow Olympics?

a)   Jürgen Hingsen

b)   Daley Thompson

c)   Steffen Grummt

4   In cricket what is the umpire signalling when he crosses both arms below his waist?

a)   Short run

b)   No-ball

c)   Dead ball

5   Which New York Yankees player was variously known as 'the Great Bambino', 'the Sultan of Swat' and 'the Colossus of Clout'?

a)   Babe Ruth

b)   Joe DiMaggio

c)   Reggie Jackson

6 Which tennis star was stabbed by a fan of a rival player during a match in Hamburg in 1993?

a) Monica Seles

b) Steffi Graf

c) Magdalena Maleeva

7 Who in 2009 became the first cyclist to win six stages of the Tour de France for 30 years?

a) Alberto Contador

b) Mark Cavendish

c) Lance Armstrong

8 Which American swimmer won a record seven medals at the 1986 world championships in Madrid?

a) Daniel Jorgensen

b) Tom Jager

c) Matt Biondi

9 Which football team did Nigel Clough manage before joining Derby County?

a) Nottingham Forest

b) Chesterfield

c) Burton Albion

10 Which cricketer made his 100th appearance for South Africa in the first Test against England in December 2009?

a) Ashwell Prince

b) Makhaya Ntini

c) Mark Boucher

1	c
2	b
3	b
4	c
5	a
6	a
7	b
8	c
9	c
10	b

MEDIUM – PART 6

1 Which country was the first to beat England's football team after their victory in the 1966 World Cup?

a) France

b) Brazil

c) Scotland

2 Who in 1992 became the oldest man to win Olympic gold in the 100m?

a) Frankie Fredericks

b) Linford Christie

c) Carl Lewis

3 In ice hockey in addition to scoring a goal and making an assist, what does a player have to do to achieve a 'Gordie Howe hat-trick'?

a) Save a penalty

b) Get into a fight

c) Get sent off

4 Why in 2010 were some Manchester United fans conducting the 'green and gold campaign', in which they wore the old colours of the club?

a) To raise money for Sport Relief

b) To protest against the owner's financial practices

c) To oppose sweatshop-produced kits

5 Which England rugby union captain was sacked – albeit briefly – in 1995 for making derogatory remarks about the game's administrators?

a) Will Carling

b) Lawrence Dallaglio

c) Phil de Glanville

6 **With which club did the former England football captain Bryan Robson begin his career?**

a) Manchester United

b) Middlesbrough

c) West Bromwich Albion

7 **Who was the first cricketer to take 700 Test wickets?**

a) Shane Warne

b) Anil Kumble

c) Muttiah Muralitharan

8 **Which boxer inflicted only the second defeat of Ricky Hatton's career when he knocked him out in May 2009?**

a) Floyd Mayweather Jr

b) Manny Pacquiao

c) Juan Manuel Márquez

9 **In which sport did Rebecca Romero win a silver medal at the 2004 Olympics prior to winning a cycling gold in Beijing?**

a) Swimming

b) Table tennis

c) Rowing

10 **In cricket who did England beat in 2009 to win the Women's World Cup for the third time?**

a) New Zealand

b) Australia

c) South Africa

A

1	c
2	b
3	b
4	b
5	a
6	c
7	a
8	b
9	c
10	a

MEDIUM – PART 7

1 Which Scottish football team normally plays its home games at Hampden Park?

a) Queen's Park

b) Hamilton Academical

c) Partick Thistle

2 Which nation in November 2009 attracted Italy's largest crowd for a home rugby union match?

a) England

b) South Africa

c) New Zealand

3 What nationality is Hicham El Guerrouj, who won the men's 1,500m and 5,000m at the 2004 Athens Olympics?

a) Ethiopian

b) Moroccan

c) Kenyan

4 In which sport to riders compete for the King's Cup, held every year in Saudi Arabia?

a) Quad bike racing

b) Camel racing

c) Cycling

5 Who was the first golfer from outside Great Britain or the USA to win the US Open?

a) Gary Player

b) Peter Thomson

c) Roberto de Vicenzo

6 **What nationality is the footballer Jean-Marc Bosman?**

a) Dutch

b) Swiss

c) Belgian

7 **Who were the opponents when England played the first cricket Test match to be held in Wales?**

a) Australia

b) Sri Lanka

c) West Indies

8 **Which former Formula One world champion announced plans to switch to the World Rally Championships after the 2009 season?**

a) Rubens Barrichello

b) Kimi Raikkonen

c) Fernando Alonso

9 **Which country in 1998 was the last to successfully defend the Davis Cup prior to Spain achieving the feat in 2009?**

a) Sweden

b) Argentina

c) USA

10 **Which city is home to the American football team known as the Bengals?**

a) Denver

b) Baltimore

c) Cincinnati

A	
1	a
2	c
3	b
4	b
5	a
6	c
7	a
8	b
9	a
10	c

MEDIUM – PART 8

1 Which cricket county did Ray Illingworth join after leaving Yorkshire in 1968?

a) Leicestershire

b) Derbyshire

c) Nottinghamshire

---

2 Which team did Nottingham Forest beat in the 1979 European Cup Final?

a) Borussia Mönchengladbach

b) Malmo

c) Bayern Munich

---

3 Which London stadium was the venue for the 1908 Olympics?

a) Wembley

b) White City

c) Crystal Palace

---

4 How many bends are there in the River Thames along the course of the University Boat Race?

a) Three

b) Four

c) Five

---

5 Which country hosted the 1962 football World Cup?

a) Brazil

b) Chile

c) Italy

6 In the athletics steeplechase what is the approximate maximum depth of the water jump?

a) 50cm (20in)

b) 60cm (24in)

c) 70cm (28in)

7 In which sport are fouls awarded for butt-ending, clipping and cross-checking?

a) Polo

b) Basketball

c) Ice hockey

8 Which NBA team did Great Britain player Ben Gordon join after leaving the Chicago Bulls?

a) Detroit Pistons

b) Houston Rockets

c) Phoenix Suns

9 Which jump jockey recorded his 2,000th winner when he rode Fighting Chance to victory at Newbury in December 2009?

a) Timmy Murphy

b) Richard Johnson

c) Ruby Walsh

10 Which former coach of the Bradford Bulls and Wigan Warriors rugby league teams joined the Celtic Crusaders after the 2009 Super League season?

a) Brian Noble

b) John Dixon

c) Jon Sharp

A

1 a

2 b

3 b

4 a

5 b

6 c

7 c

8 a

9 b

10 a

Q MEDIUM – PART 9

1 Which postwar Olympic Games was the first to be shown on television?

a) 1948

b) 1952

c) 1956

2 What was the name of Scunthorpe United's home ground before they moved to Glanford Park?

a) County Ground

b) Old Show Ground

c) Victoria Ground

3 Which athlete won 122 consecutive 400m hurdles races between 1977 and 1987?

a) Harald Schmid

b) Ed Moses

c) Danny Harris

4 How many modes of dismissal are there in cricket?

a) Seven

b) Ten

c) Twelve

5 What sort of event was Running Deer, held at the Olympics from 1908 to 1924?

a) Long distance running

b) Shooting

c) Canoeing

6 **Which former England footballer managed the Ireland team at the 1990 and 1994 World Cups?**

a) Trevor Brooking

b) Bryan Robson

c) Jack Charlton

7 **Which rugby union club refused to play a Guinness Premiership game at Sale in December 2009 because they claimed the pitch was dangerous?**

a) Wasps

b) London Irish

c) Northampton

8 **In which sport did the former Irish Olympic shot put competitor Victor Costello win 39 caps for his country?**

a) Hurling

b) Rugby league

c) Rugby union

9 **Which British driver completed the triple crown of motor racing when he won the Le Mans 24-hour race in 1972 to add to the Monaco Grand Prix and the Indianapolis 500?**

a) Graham Hill

b) Jackie Stewart

c) James Hunt

10 **Which Pakistan fast bowler became known as the Rawalpindi Express?**

a) Wasim Akram

b) Waqar Younis

c) Shoaib Akhtar

A

1	a
2	b
3	b
4	b
5	b
6	c
7	a
8	c
9	a
10	c

MEDIUM – PART 10

1   With which NBA side did the Great Britain basketball player Luol Deng make his name?

a)   Utah Jazz

b)   Boston Celtics

c)   Chicago Bulls

2   Which nation made its Winter Olympics debut at Cortina d'Ampezzo, Italy, in 1956?

a)   Soviet Union

b)   Italy

c)   Netherlands

3   In squash, what colour dot signifies the fastest ball?

a)   Green

b)   Yellow

c)   Blue

4   For what reason did Michael Angelow hit the headlines at Lord's in August 1975?

a)   Streaking

b)   Hit by the ball

c)   Scored a century

5   Against which country did former England rugby union coach Andy Robinson make his coaching debut for Scotland?

a)   Argentina

b)   Fiji

c)   Canada

GENERAL KNOWLEDGE ★★

6 Which was the first Football League team to be managed by Darren Ferguson, son of Sir Alex?

a) Walsall

b) Milton Keynes Dons

c) Peterborough United

7 Which port marks the finishing point of the Fastnet Race?

a) Plymouth

b) Portsmouth

c) Bournemouth

8 Which country did volleyball player Jason Haldane represent before being cleared to play for Great Britain?

a) Ireland

b) Canada

c) Australia

9 In which sport did the South Korean Peter Suk coach British performers for four years until stepping down after the 2009 World Cup Grand Final?

a) Table tennis

b) Taekwondo

c) Archery

10 Which Premier League striker was suspended for three matches after admitting he threw a coin at Burnley fans during a Carling Cup game in 2008?

a) Michael Owen

b) Didier Drogba

c) Fernando Torres

A

1 c
2 a
3 c
4 a
5 b
6 c
7 a
8 b
9 c
10 b

HARD – PART 1

---

1 From what bridge does the University Boat Race start?

a) Barnes

b) Putney

c) Chiswick

---

2 In which decade did Lester Piggott first win the Derby?

a) 1950s

b) 1960s

c) 1970s

---

3 Who was the first player to score a maximum break in the World Snooker Championships?

a) Cliff Thorburn

b) Eddie Charlton

c) Ray Reardon

---

4 Which pop superstar is the nephew of Roy Dwight, who suffered a broken leg playing for Nottingham Forest in the 1959 FA Cup final?

a) Rod Stewart

b) Sting

c) Elton John

---

5 Who qualified for the British Men's Chess Championships in 1977, three days before his 12th birthday, and went on to win the title in 1984, 1987 and 1998?

a) Nigel Short

b) Michael Adams

c) David Howell

6 **Where did Roger Bannister run the first sub-four-minute mile in 1954?**

a) Cambridge

b) Oxford

c) White City

7 **In which area of London did Arsenal play their first-ever home game?**

a) Plumstead

b) Woolwich

c) Islington

8 **In what year were the Winter Olympics first held two years after the Summer Games rather than in the same year?**

a) 1992

b) 1994

c) 1996

9 **Whose statue is outside the Olympic Stadium in Helsinki?**

a) Hannes Kolehmainen

b) Emil Zatopek

c) Paavo Nurmi

10 **Who became the first bowls world champion in 1966?**

a) Malwyn Evans

b) Doug Watson

c) David Bryant

A

1 b

2 a

3 a

4 c

5 a

6 b

7 a

8 b

9 c

10 c

HARD – PART 2

1 The oldest competitor at the 2008 Beijing Olympics, Hiroshi Hoketsu, competed in which event?

a) Dressage

b) Archery

c) Shooting

2 Which county cricket club did Brian Close join after leaving Yorkshire?

a) Durham

b) Leicestershire

c) Somerset

3 In which city did the British diver Tom Daley win the 10m platform event at the 2009 FINA World Championships?

a) Rome

b) Milan

c) Florence

4 Who resigned as coach of the England rugby league team after their defeat against Australia in the 2009 Four Nations championship?

a) Brian Smith

b) Tony Smith

c) Brian Noble

5 Which South American football team play their home games at La Bombonera?

a) Boca Juniors

b) Peñarol

c) Estudiantes

6 In which sport did Robert Mackay, a former inmate of a debtors' prison, become the first world champion in 1820?

a) Croquet

b) Real tennis

c) Rackets

7 Which sporting trophy is affectionately known as 'the Auld Mug'?

a) The Calcutta Cup

b) The America's Cup

c) The FA Cup

8 In which Spanish city in 2009 did Garry Kasparov and Anatoly Karpov renew a chess rivalry that began during the 1980s?

a) Madrid

b) Valencia

c) Barcelona

9 Which island hosts the annual World Rugby Classic for veteran union players?

a) Jersey

b) Hong Kong

c) Bermuda

10 Who was Bill Shankly's predecessor as manager of Liverpool?

a) Don Welsh

b) Phil Taylor

c) Andy Beattie

A

1 a
2 c
3 a
4 b
5 a
6 c
7 b
8 b
9 c
10 b

HARD – PART 3

1 On a dartboard which number is directly opposite the number 1?

a) 12

b) 15

c) 19

2 Which rugby Test-playing nation did Nick Mallett coach from 1997 until 2000?

a) Ireland

b) Argentina

c) South Africa

3 How many gold medals did the Great Britain team win at the Beijing Olympics?

a) 19

b) 23

c) 25

4 Which Japanese city was due to host the cancelled 1940 Winter Olympics?

a) Yokohama

b) Nagano

c) Sapporo

5 What is the name of the line drawn across a snooker table?

a) Foul

b) Base

c) Baulk

6 As defending champion, which golfer selected Welsh lamb for the US Masters champions' dinner?

a) Nick Faldo

b) Ian Woosnam

c) Sandy Lyle

7 In the Euro 1976 football championship Wales topped their group in the qualifing round. Which stage did they eventually reach?

a) Quarter-finals

b) Semi-finals

c) The final

8 Who in 2008 became the youngest driver to win a Formula One grand prix?

a) Sebastian Vettel

b) Jenson Button

c) Jarno Trulli

9 Which horse in 2008 became the first filly to win the Prix de l'Arc de Triomphe for 15 years?

a) Dylan Thomas

b) Zarkava

c) Sea the Stars

10 Which footballer made a record with the pop group Lindisfarne?

a) Paul Gascoigne

b) Kevin Keegan

c) Alan Shearer

A	
1	c
2	c
3	a
4	c
5	c
6	b
7	a
8	a
9	b
10	a

HARD – PART 4

1 At which cricket ground did batsman Brian Lara achieve his record run total of 501?

a) Edgbaston

b) Old Trafford

c) Taunton

2 What nationality was Oscar Swahn, who won his first Olympic medal for shooting in 1908 at the age of 60?

a) Dutch

b) German

c) Swedish

3 Which runner was the first man to be ranked at world number one for the 200m and 400m?

a) Alberto Juantorena

b) Quincy Watts

c) Michael Johnson

4 In which sport did Guido Cappellini win his first world title in 1993?

a) Rallying

b) Powerboat racing

c) Hang gliding

5 Who held the men's 200m world record for 17 years?

a) Pietro Mennea

b) Walter Dix

c) Carl Lewis

★ ★ ★

6 Evan Noel and John Jacob Astor were gold medallists at the 1908 London Olympics in which sport that has never returned to the Games?

a) Croquet

b) Rackets

c) Lacrosse

7 Who partnered Simon Archer to a silver badminton medal at the 1999 world championships and a bronze at the 2000 Sydney Olympics?

a) Gail Emms

b) Donna Kellogg

c) Joanne Goode

8 Which jockey won 1,699 races, the most in the UK over fences, until Tony McCoy overtook him in 2002?

a) Richard Dunwoody

b) Peter Scudamore

c) John Francome

9 Which British long distance runner was known for his distinctive red socks?

a) Brendan Foster

b) David Bedford

c) David Moorcroft

10 Who finished as top scorer with ten goals at the 1970 football World Cup in Mexico?

a) Jairzinho

b) Teófilo Cubillas

c) Gerd Müller

A

1 a

2 c

3 c

4 b

5 a

6 b

7 c

8 a

9 b

10 c

HARD – PART 5

1 Which team was the last to qualify for the 2010 football World Cup?

a) Uruguay

b) New Zealand

c) Cameroon

2 Which English bowler was hit for six consecutive sixes in an over by Yuvraj Singh in a Twenty20 match in September 2007?

a) Chris Tremlett

b) Liam Plunkett

c) Stuart Broad

3 Why was Swedish wrestler Ara Abrahamian stripped of his bronze medal at the Beijing Olympics?

a) He failed a drugs test

b) He started a fight after the bout had finished

c) He discarded his medal in protest at the judging

4 In men's volleyball how high is the net?

a) 1.83m (6ft)

b) 2.44m (8ft)

c) 3.05m (10ft)

5 Which famous rider partnered Stroller to showjumping success in the 1967 Hickstead Derby and also won silver at the 1968 Olympics?

a) Marion Coakes

b) David Broome

c) Harvey Smith

6 **Which world heavyweight boxing champion was christened Arnold Cream?**

a) Ezzard Charles

b) Joe Louis

c) Jersey Joe Walcott

7 **Who was the first European jockey to win the Belmont Stakes?**

a) Michael Kinane

b) Lester Piggott

c) Joe Mercer

8 **Who was the first snooker player to win the amateur and professional world titles?**

a) John Higgins

b) Graeme Dott

c) Ken Doherty

9 **Which player scored the fastest goal in FA Cup final history after 25 seconds of the 2009 clash between Everton and Chelsea?**

a) Didier Drogba

b) Louis Saha

c) Tim Cahill

10 **How many nations competed at the first modern Olympics in 1896?**

a) 10

b) 12

c) 14

GENERAL KNOWLEDGE ★★★

A

1	a
2	c
3	c
4	b
5	a
6	c
7	a
8	c
9	b
10	c

HARD – PART 6

1 Which player scored a pair on his Test debut against Australia in 1975, but bounced back to become one of England's greatest batsmen?

a) Graham Gooch

b) David Gower

c) Graeme Hick

2 English-born footballer Chris Birchall has played for Port Vale, Coventry City and LA Galaxy, but which national side did he represent?

a) USA

b) Bermuda

c) Trinidad and Tobago

3 In which event did the American Charles Jewtraw win the first gold medal at the inaugural Winter Olympics in 1924?

a) Men's downhill skiing

b) Luge

c) Speed skating

4 In sailing, what is signified by displaying a blue and white chequered flag?

a) Recall of a particular boat

b) All racing abandoned

c) Ten minutes to start

5 In which aquatic event did Britain's Sara Campbell set a world record in April 2009?

a) Synchronised swimming

b) Platform diving

c) Freediving

6 Which gymnast became British women's champion in 2009 after winning three of the four categories?

a) Becky Downie

b) Rebecca Wing

c) Beth Tweddle

7 For which country did sprinter Susanthika Jayasinghe win a first Olympic medal with bronze in the 200m at the 2000 Games?

a) Sri Lanka

b) Philippines

c) Singapore

8 What nationality is Kwame Nkrumah-Acheampong, who became his country's first skier to qualify for the Winter Olympics?

a) South African

b) Nigerian

c) Ghanaian

9 Which side did the England netball team beat for the first time since the early 1980s in the World Netball Series in Manchester in 2009?

a) Australia

b) New Zealand

c) France

10 What size engines will be used in MotoGP from 2012 as a result of the 2009 agreement between the event's governing body and the major manufacturers?

a) 800cc

b) 990cc

c) 1,000cc

A	
1	a
2	c
3	c
4	b
5	c
6	a
7	a
8	c
9	a
10	c

HARD – PART 7

1 At which Olympics did British rower Jack Beresford win his fifth consecutive medal?

a) Amsterdam, 1928

b) Los Angeles, 1932

c) Berlin, 1936

2 What differentiates a goalkeeper in bandy from his counterpart in ice hockey?

a) No stick

b) No skates

c) Different colour stick

3 Which country hosted the first Commonwealth Games in 1930?

a) England

b) Canada

c) India

4 Against which team did David Beckham make his England debut in 1996?

a) Moldova

b) Jamaica

c) Spain

5 Which England batsman scored his 100th first-class century in an Ashes Test at Headingley in 1977?

a) John Edrich

b) Dennis Amiss

c) Geoff Boycott

6   How old was Ian Thorpe when he won his first gold medal at the 2000 Olympics?

a)   17 years

b)   18 years

c)   19 years

7   In which sport would you find strokers, crankers and even helicopter deliveries?

a)   Hurling

b)   Baseball

c)   Ten pin bowling

8   Which country won Olympic gold at lacrosse in 1904 and 1908, the only years that the sport featured in the programme?

a)   USA

b)   Canada

c)   France

9   Who scored a maximum break in the quarter-finals of the 2009 World Snooker Championships?

a)   Stephen Hendry

b)   Ronnie O'Sullivan

c)   Ding Junhui

10   Which racehorse won an unprecedented fourth Ascot Gold Cup in June 2009?

a)   Ouija Board

b)   Yeats

c)   Allegretto

A

1   c

2   a

3   b

4   a

5   c

6   a

7   c

8   b

9   a

10   b

HARD – PART 8

GENERAL KNOWLEDGE

★ ★ ★

1 In which event did Jure Franko win Yugoslavia's only medal when Sarajevo hosted the 1984 Winter Olympics?

a) Luge singles

b) Giant slalom

c) 5,000m speed skating

2 In cricket how much time does an incoming batsman have to reach the crease before he risks being timed out?

a) Three minutes

b) Four minutes

c) Five minutes

3 Which team finished the 2008–9 season as British Basketball League champions?

a) Everton Tigers

b) Sheffield Sharks

c) Newcastle Eagles

4 Against which cricket touring team in 1992 did the umpire and former bowler Neil Mallender win his two England Test caps?

a) Pakistan

b) India

c) Zimbabwe

5 Which football team did West Ham United beat in the 1965 European Cup Winners' Cup final?

a) TSV Munich 1860

b) Hannover 96

c) Schalke 04

6 **The USA and which other country dominated swimming events at the 1976 Olympics, winning 13 and 11 gold medals respectively?**

a) Soviet Union

b) East Germany

c) Australia

7 **Which team did England beat to win the 2009 European team squash championships?**

a) France

b) Spain

c) Bulgaria

8 **Which player gave Scotland a shock lead in the 1982 football World Cup game against Brazil before the South Americans recovered to win the game 4–1?**

a) Gordon Strachan

b) John Wark

c) David Narey

9 **How did the England netball player Rachel Dunn make history in the 2009 World Netball Series tie against Samoa after the introduction of the Fast Net rules?**

a) First player to be fouled out

b) First rolling substitute

c) Scored the first four-point goal

10 **Who in 1977 replaced Cliff Morgan in the first change of a captain on the BBC TV quiz show *A Question of Sport*?**

a) Emlyn Hughes

b) Brendan Foster

c) Bill Beaumont

A

1	b
2	a
3	c
4	a
5	a
6	b
7	a
8	c
9	c
10	b

HARD – PART 9

1   Against which nation did Indian cricket player Sachin Tendulkar win his first Test match cap in 1989?

a)   Pakistan

b)   Sri Lanka

c)   West Indies

2   What nationality was Christa Luding-Rothenburger, who in 1988 became the first person to win Winter and Summer Olympic medals in the same year?

a)   Swiss

b)   Czech

c)   East German

3   In which racket sport did Australian Robert Fahey win the world title for a record ninth time in 2006?

a)   Rackets

b)   Real tennis

c)   Badminton

4   In 2009, which British bowls player won the men's singles world title and partnered David Gourlay to the indoor doubles world title?

a)   Billy Jackson

b)   Robert Weale

c)   Mervyn King

5   The 1994 Winter Olympics were the first to take place in a different year from the Summer Olympics. Where were they held?

a)   Lillehammer

b)   Albertville

c)   Nagano

6 In greyhound racing which number trap houses the dog with the black and white striped jacket?

a) Trap 1

b) Trap 4

c) Trap 6

7 In which sport did Paul Drinkhall win men's singles, men's doubles and mixed doubles titles at the 2009 English National Championships in Sheffield?

a) Pool

b) Billiards

c) Table tennis

8 Which nation was the first to win the women's Rugby World Cup?

a) New Zealand

b) England

c) USA

9 Who in 1954 was the first winner of the BBC Sports Personality of the Year Award?

a) Jim Laker

b) Chris Chataway

c) Dai Rees

10 Which javelin thrower won a gold medal at the 1987 World Athletics Championships but never won Olympic gold, managing bronze in 1984 and having to settle for silver in 1988?

a) Tessa Sanderson

b) Fatima Whitbread

c) Sue Howland

1	a
2	c
3	b
4	a
5	a
6	c
7	c
8	c
9	b
10	b

HARD – PART 10

1 Which country was banned from taking part in team sports at the 1992 Barcelona Olympics?

a) Zimbabwe

b) Yugoslavia

c) China

---

2 In which sport do players compete for the MacRobertson Shield?

a) Croquet

b) Eton fives

c) Rugby union

---

3 Which team in 1929 became the first European nation to beat the England football team?

a) Spain

b) Hungary

c) Italy

---

4 Which cyclist won the women's British National Road Race in 2009?

a) Nicole Cooke

b) Victoria Pendleton

c) Catherine Williamson

---

5 Sweden's Kerstin Palm was the first woman to compete at seven Olympic Games. In which sport did she compete?

a) Rowing

b) Equestrianism

c) Fencing

6 In which sport did Talandracas beat Enigma to win the 2009 Prince of Wales Trophy?

a) Lacrosse

b) Polo

c) Real tennis

7 Which world record was set by Alan Pettigrew on the island of Inchmurrin, Loch Lomond, in August 1984?

a) Haggis hurling

b) Fell walking

c) Caber tossing

8 At which major tennis championship does the winner of the women's singles receive the Venus Rosewater Dish?

a) Wimbledon

b) US Open

c) Australian Open

9 How many runs did Don Bradman need to secure a career batting average of 100 when he was bowled for a duck in his last Test match innings in 1948?

a) Four

b) Six

c) Ten

10 How many points are scored from the black ball during a maximum break in snooker?

a) 77

b) 105

c) 112

A

1	b
2	a
3	a
4	a
5	c
6	b
7	a
8	a
9	a
10	c